Book Collecting

The cover of this book has been adapted from a title-page designed by Dürer about 1513

To
A.F. Wallis

A sixteenth-century printing shop showing a printer screwing down a press; an assistant inking a forme; another assistant bringing in paper; an apprentice stacking printed sheets; the master overseeing operations.

Book Collecting

A GUIDE TO ANTIQUARIAN AND SECONDHAND BOOKS

by

Stephen Miller

Provincial Booksellers Fairs Association

Published by Stephen Miller &
Provincial Booksellers Fairs Association
The Old Coach House, 16 Melbourn Street,
Royston, Hertfordshire, SG8 7BZ.

Tel: 01763 248400
Fax: 01763 248921

ISBN 09524122-17

British Library Cataloguing in Publication Data.
A catalogue record for this book is available
from the British Library.

Typeset in Monotype Baskerville® by Gina Dolan, P.B.F.A.
Printed and bound by Biddles Ltd, Guildford

Contents

Introduction

This is a book about books, secondhand and antiquarian. It is written for the person who probably already takes an interest in old books, as reader or collector, or perhaps as embryo dealer, and who wants to know more about them.

It provides an introduction to all the main subject areas - a glance at the List of Contents will indicate what is covered.

The basics of the book are explained, as well as the jargon of the trade. Guidance is given on how to set about appraising books, on values and valuations, and on such questions as why one copy of a work should be worth more, or less, than another.

The book doesn't claim to be the 'bible of book collecting'. Each area is covered in outline only. For those who wish to pursue a particular interest there is, in most cases, a large body of specialist literature available. At the end of the book there is a list of works the reader can consult if he or she wants to follow up a particular field of enquiry.

The term 'collecting' is rather vague, covering as it does a wide range of activities. I use it as a shorthand term to embrace all types of secondhand and antiquarian book-buying - the casual purchase of a volume, the dedicated pursuit of titles in a particular field, the putting together of a library of the most expensive and important books.

'Antiquarian' is similarly vague. There is no date line with old books beyond which a book is by definition 'antiquarian'. 'Antiquarian bookseller' may include, for some purposes, dealers who specialise in modern first editions, perhaps nothing printed before the Second World War. In this book no attempt is made to draw a rigid line between secondhand and antiquarian. Nevertheless, there are important differences between books produced at different times. Discussion of these differences will occur naturally in the relevant chapter.

Printing to 1800

In this introductory chapter I shall provide a summary overview of the history of printing from the beginnings up to the end of the eighteenth century. This period of roughly 350 years may be called the time of the hand-made book, when book production in all its branches remained largely a craft. From the early nineteenth century onwards mechanisation began to be introduced into one branch after another until by the middle of the century the craft element had been all but eliminated. There are three main strands to this overview: (1) a sketch of what is involved in the process of casting letter-type in metal; (2) an outline of some of the early developments in the design of letter-type; (3) brief details of some of the most important early printers and type designers.

This emphasis on letter-type - its manufacture and design - is justified by the fact that the early history of printing is, from a purely technical point of view, largely the history of the invention of casting type in metal and the subsequent development of letter forms. The principle of the press was already well known, and the printing press remained basically unaltered in its structure and operation until the invention of machine printing in the nineteenth century. Paper - the subject of the next chapter - was already being manufactured, and the operations involved likewise remained broadly unchanged until the late eighteenth century (though this is obviously not to say that there wasn't great variety in the type and quality of different papers); and while different types of ink were developed to suit the new process, again there was nothing new in the principles involved. The one new invention crucial to the whole business was that of casting type in metal, and once this invention was established it is to the evolution of letter forms and the art of the type designer and punch-cutter that we must look for an understanding of how printing developed during the first three centuries and a half of its existence.

Little is known of the first printing presses, though illustrations in early books give some idea of their general appearance (see frontis. illustration). The principle of the screw press was already well known, with its application in agriculture (pressing grapes and olives), in the printing of designs on cloth and even in paper manufacture. Its adaptation to printing from type must have been a relatively straightforward matter. Simplifying somewhat, the main component would be a wooden frame which held the platen at the end of a screw and enclosed the bed of the press. The frame would be of very stout construction given the pressures involved and also to ensure an even pressure of the platen on the paper. Some contemporary illustrations even show the frame braced against the ceiling. The block of type would be laid on the bed of the press, to one edge of which was attached by hinges a flat plate called a tympan. The paper to be printed would be laid on the tympan. Once the block of type was in place it would be inked and the tympan, with the paper in place, laid down over it. The platen would then be screwed down to force the paper to take the impression. After this operation the platen would be raised, the tympan lifted and the paper removed. The block of type would then be inked again and the operation repeated.

Printing from a wooden block was a technique known long before the invention of printing from metal type, though its use was confined largely to the reproduction of illustrations rather than text. A design would be cut out of the block of wood, the portions left in relief inked over and then pressed onto the paper - by hand rather than in a press - to produce the impression. By the mid-fifteenth century it was common practice to add to the illustration a few lines of text. A series of sheets thus printed - on one side of the sheet only and frequently hand-coloured after printing - would then be bound together, to produce what is now known as a **block book**. The most elaborate examples of text produced by this method are the work of Dutch printers active just before the invention of printing proper in the fifteenth century. Works of devotion and school books were the most common productions.

The primitive nature of this method of printing is obvious. The equivalent of each page had to be cut as a single unit, within which each individual letter was cut. Moreover, each letter could only be used once. When the same letter was required for another page it had to be cut again. The core problem to be overcome - what the invention of printing was all about - was the discovery of a method of manufacturing individual letter-types in quantity which could be used over and over again to print different words in different sentences in different books.

The solution to the problem involved casting letter-type in metal. Once the mould had been made, an almost indefinite number of type could be cast from it. Not only was it possible to produce large quantities of type, but each example of a given letter would be virtually the same as the others. And metal being hard-wearing, the type could be used many times over.

The first stage in the making of type involves the manufacture of a punch, a billet of steel on the end of which the letter has been engraved or cut in relief (and reversed from left to right). With letters such as *a*, *e* and *o*, which contain an enclosed space, a preliminary stage could involve the inner contour of the letter being first cut on the end of a counter- punch, which would then be driven into the end of the punch proper. The outer contour of the letter would then be cut. Once the punch is complete the steel is hardened then stamped into a soft metal such as copper to form a matrix. The matrix is set in a mould and molten metal poured in. When the molten metal has hardened the result is a piece of letter-type. A complete alphabet of types, together with both large and small letters, numerals, accents, punctuation marks and so forth is known as a **fount** (font) or **face**.

This is no more than a sketch of the theory. The practice involves a great deal more. For example, one crucial aspect of the matter is the spacing between letters; these spaces are in some ways as important as the letters themselves. The whole effort of the type designer is directed towards the production of a fount which, as well as being suited for the particular printing job in hand, is at once pleasing in itself and easy to read, in the sense that the eye flows over the text. (The challenge may be compared to that of composing film music: the music should complement the film but not intrude; the audience should be aware of the music only subconsciously.)

The details of letter design are far beyond the scope of this work but it is worth mentioning several of the more important constituents of the letter.

An **ascender** is that part of a letter which ascends above the main body; thus, the letter 'h' has an ascender, and is an ascending letter, while the letter 'n' has no ascender. The letter 'y', by contrast, has a **descender** and is known as a descending letter. The **serif** is the small finishing stroke at the top or bottom of the main body of the letter. A **kern** is that part of a letter which *overhangs* the main body; the letter 'f' is an example of a letter with a kern.

All early designs of letter used in printing were based on the written letter, and the characteristics of the written letter of the time are reflected in the letter design. The normal writing tool was a square-ended pen, which produced a variety of thicknesses depending on the angle at which it was drawn across the paper. The hand would work at an angle to the paper, hence the presence of oblique strokes. The serif is a characteristic of the written letter adopted by the designers of type.

Type is nowadays measured by the **point**. One point is equal to 0.01383 of an inch. Type sizes are all multiples of this figure. For example, a 72-point type measures 0.9962 of an inch (a very large type indeed). A relatively recent practice is for the printer or publisher to give details of the fount used in the printing of a book. The name of the fount will be preceded by the point size, eg., '12-point Monotype Caslon'. (This book is printed in 12-point Monotype Baskerville). Most books are printed in type sizes ranging betwen 9-point and 12-point. Originally the name of a book, the term **pica** has since come to be used to designate a certain type-size (on the basis that this size of type was always used for that book). Pica is equal to 12 points. Two other similarly traditional names for type-sizes which are occasionally met with are **nonpareil** for 6-point and **bourgeois** for 9-point.

The process of casting type by hand remained largely unchanged in its principles for four hundred years. Although the technology of mechanical type-casting was known in the seventeenth century, it was not until the nineteenth that machines for the purpose were built and commercially operated. More recently still, with the appearance of computers and related technology, the physical metal type has all but disappeared from the printing process.

With a fount successfully cast what the printer now had to work with was a collection of movable type, that is, a collection of letter-type that could be moved around at will, combined and recombined for different printing jobs. **Composition** is the term used to describe the process of putting the individual types together to form a block of type which will print a complete page of text. The block of type is locked into a frame called a **chase**. In traditional composition the capital letters would be held in one case and the small letters in another. The case containing the capitals would always be placed above that containing the small letters, possibly because the compositor was always using more small letters than capitals and therefore needed the case containing the former within easier reach. Whatever the reason, this disposition of the cases has led to capital letters often being referred to as **upper-case** letters and small letters as **lower-case**. As with type-casting, the principles of composing by hand remained largely unchanged until well into the nineteenth century, when machines began to be employed.

Johann **Gutenberg** (1400-1468) is the one printer whose name is familiar to virtually everyone. Gutenberg, who was trained as a goldsmith, is generally credited with the invention of casting type in metal. There are some who question the attribution but what cannot be questioned is that the process was at least brought to perfection under Gutenberg's authority. His Bible, printed at Mainz probably in 1456, is the first great masterpiece of printing. Paradoxically, given the very quality of the production, it isn't unreasonable to assume that this was not the first attempt at printing from movable type; the technique must have been exercised on other works, but virtually nothing is known of any such.

There are some bibliographers who argue that Gutenberg's role in the printing of the Bible was little more than supervisory, with much of the actual work being undertaken by his assistants. Whatever the degree of Gutenberg's involvement in the project, it certainly represents the high-point in his career as a printer. Soon afterwards he became involved in a number of law suits to do with debts as a result of which he lost much of his equipment, including his types.

Much of Gutenberg's equipment was acquired by his former financial backer, one Johann **Furst**, who promptly set up in business with Gutenberg's assistant, Peter **Schoeffer**. Together they printed and published a number of books, including a Psalter which has the distinction of being the first printed book to carry both the date of printing (1457) and the place (Mainz).

As we have already seen, the first printers looked to contemporary hand-writing to provide them with a model on which to base their designs of type. As the first motor cars (horseless carriages) were designed to look like that

Quod cū audisset david: descendit in
presidiū. Philistijm autem venientes
diffusi sunt in valle raphaim. Et cō-
suluit david dn̄m dicens. Si ascendā
ad philistijm· et si dabis eos ī manu
mea? Et dixit dn̄s ad david. Ascende:
q̄a tradens dabo philistijm in manu
tua. Venit ergo david ad baalphara-
sim: et percussit eos ibi et dixit. Divisit
dn̄s inimicos meos corā me: sicut di-
vidunt aque. Propterea vocatū ē no-
men loci illiꝰ baalpharasim. Et reliq̄-
runt ibi sculptilia sua: q̄ tulit david et
viri eiꝰ. Et addiderunt adhuc philisti-
im ut ascenderent: et diffusi sūt ī valle
raphaim. Cōsuluit autē david dn̄m.
Si ascendā cōtra philisteos: ⁊ tradas
eos in manus meas? Qui rn̄dit. Nō
ascendas cōtra eos sed gira post tergū
eorū: ⁊ venies ad eos ex adūso pirorū.
Et cū audieris sonitū clamoris gra-
dientis ī cacumīe piroꝝ tūc inibis p̄liū:
q̄a tūc egredietur dn̄s āte faciē tuā: ut p-

Gothic type: a specimen from Gutenberg's Bible (c.1456)

which they were replacing (carriages), so the first printers designed their type in imitation of existing book hands (the style of hand-writing of the scribes).

Most early type designs fall into one of two categories, **gothic** or **roman**. By gothic is meant, roughly, the book hand characteristic of medieval Europe, often known in England as **black letter**. It is the kind of script still occasionally seen advertising 'olde worlde' attractions, pubs, antique shops and tea shops. In printing, a variety of it was still in use in Germany until the end of the Second World War. One of Hitler's decrees as soon as he assumed power was to the effect that all printing in the country should employ gothic faces as gothic was deemed more truly 'germanic'. The gothic type is characterised by its angularity and stiffness, by the number of ornamental flourishes to the letters and by its thick, black appearance on the page, an appearance quite alien to modern eyes.

There are numerous different types of gothic, the result of different printers working in different cities and countries, each with its own model book hand, and each printer often striving to improve upon the type face in implicit recognition that it was not very satisfactory for much book work. The three main subdivisions within the gothic type are known respectively as 'lettre de forme', 'lettre de somme' and 'lettre batarde'. In the late nineteenth century William Morris revived the gothic type for a number of books from his Kelmscott Press.

Within two or three decades of Gutenberg's Bible of 1456, the new invention had spread from Germany to most of the cities of Europe. It is worth recalling that the Europe of the time was a very cosmopolitan place, with people of all nationalities and occupations travelling the length and breadth of the Continent in search of work or distraction. Often this nomadic tendency was the result of social unrest or war, but often it was quite spontaneous. Trade was another spur to migration and movement betwen countries, and the printing trade was no exception. Printers frequently moved from one country to another; they would exchange stocks of type as well as expertise; they would export part of an edition of a work to a second city or country, where it would generally appear with a different title-page. Wood blocks used to produce illustrations were also traded freely.

While the Bible of Gutenberg was a lavish production, involving great expense and effort, and consequently selling for a very high sum, other printers were quick to exploit the new invention to service the mass market.

Lettres de Forme.

Quesitũ ē ex parte
tua si cõmutationes
fieri valeant preben-
dar: cũ commutatio
dignitatum in turoñ
concilio fuerit inter-
dicta. Generaliter i-
taq teneas q cõmu-
tationes prebendar
de iure fieri nõ pñt
pserti cũ pactiõe pm-
issa: q circa spũalia
vl cõnexa spũalibus

Ancienne Batarde.

En telle mesure que
vous mesurerez, on vo9
mesurera. Et pourquoy
regarde tu le festu en
loeil de ton frere & tu ne
vois point une poultre
qui est en ton oeil. Ou
comment dis tu a ton frere,
frere permetz que ie tire
hors de tõ oeil ung festu
& voicy une poultre est
en ton oeil. Hypocrite,
iecte premierement la
poultre hors de ton oeil
& adoncques tu verras a
tirer le festu hors d loeil
de ton frere.

Lettres de Somme.

Ad nostram noueris audientiam per-
uenisse quod cum .R. laicus lator presen-
tium ab. M. mutuum recipere voluis-
set: creditor ne per canonẽ cõtra vsura-
rios editum posset in posterum cõueniri
domos & oliuas recepit ab eodẽ titulo
emptionis: cum reuera cunctus vsura-
ri9 ageret: quod patet ex eo quod creditor
debitori promisit quod quicumque a sep-
tẽnio vsque ad nouẽnium daret. lx. vn-
cias tarẽorum quẽ vix dimidiã iusti pre-
tii contingebãt domos eius restitueret
& oliuas.

The three principal categories of gothic letter - Forme, Batarde and Somme - reworked in the eighteenth century by Fournier

One of the world's first 'best-sellers' was the *Nuremburg Chronicle* printed in that city by Anton Koberger in 1493. This Chronicle was a combined history, geography and mythology and was illustrated with almost two thousand wood cut illustrations. In what was to become a typical practice of printers throughout Europe over the next two hunded years, many of these illustrations were used several times over to represent entirely different scenes. This practice raises the interesting question - which I won't be discussing here - of the difference between illustration and ornament, the former intended to inform, the latter to decorate, or as some might say, distract.

Accompanying the dispersion of the new invention was a great deal of imaginative thinking on type design. In particular, there was a recognition that gothic types were unsatisfactory in many ways. One result of this thinking was the development of roman type. This was derived from a script used at the time of the late Roman empire, one which was preserved during the time of Charlemagne, from which is derived another name for it, 'carolingian'. The roman type is effectively the type face with which we are familiar today.

Aldus Manutius (c.1450-1515) was one of the most important early printers to utilise roman types. He lived and worked in Venice which, after Germany, was the most important centre of early printing. It is reasonable to assume that a significant influence upon his thinking in type design was the humanistic tradition of northern Italy, which may be contrasted with the medieval culture of north and central Europe. The clash between gothic and roman types is sometimes characterised as a struggle between medieval northern Europe and the south of the Renaissance. It is true that gothic types persisted in use a great deal longer in the conservative north of the Continent. What is also true is that where the two co-existed, gothic tended to be reserved for works of theology, law and similar 'serious' subjects, while roman was employed for books of belles lettres, verse and editions of the classics.

Aldus - whose name lives on in the adjective **aldine** - was typical of early printers in the manner in which he combined a variety of functions which nowadays are quite separate. He was a publisher, interested in producing books; he was a bookseller, selling his own productions. But he was at the same time a printer, organising and supervising the printing of his own books, and it is for this that he is probably best remembered today. In addition, he was concerned with the design of the type used in his books, commissioning the production of a variety of founts for different purposes. One of his most

Itaq; ,quas pueri miſerimus ad te lucubra
tiones noſtras ; numerare aliquas poſſu-
mus; quas adoleſcentes, non poſſumus :
quo in conſilio nobis diutius permanen
dum eſſe non puto: nam ut interdum nõ
loqui moderati hominis eſt; ſic ſemper
ſilere cum eo , quem diligas, perignaui:
neq; Hercule; ſi in officio permanſimus
in prima aetate ; debemùs nunc , tanq̃
inexercitati hiſtriones , in ſecundo , aut
tertio actu corruiſſe. praeſertim cum
aemulatio tuorum ſtudiorum Angele
nos non excitare modo languentes poſſit,
ſed etiam incendere ;quippe , qui multa,
et praeclara habuimus a te ſemper, habe
múſq; quotidie et conſuetudinis noſtrae
teſtimonia , et doctrinae tuae. Quare ſi
cuti pueri ſcriptiunculas noſtras, quaſi la
ctentis ingenii acerbitatem , detulimus
ad te; ſic nunc deinceps etiam ad te adole
ſcentiae noſtrae primos foetus deferemus;
non quo me ipſe plus ames: nam iam id

Roman type: Aldus's design as used in Petro Bembo's "De Aetna" (1495)

famous roman founts came to be known as **Bembo**, after Pietro Bembo (1470-1547), poet and cardinal, in one of whose books the type was first used. Many printers today offer varieties of Bembo in their type-specimen catalogues.

A further type of book hand was known as **chancery**. Unlike the rather formal gothic and roman, chancery tended to be reserved for the more prosaic purposes of everyday life - legal documents, business correspondence and the like. In some respects chancery resembles our own idea of handwriting, in particular with its forward slant. Aldus took this book hand as the model for a completely different design of type, which became known as **italic**. The italic we are familiar with today is little altered since Aldus' version first appeared some 500 years ago. One of the great advantages of italic was that it leant itself to use in small format editions, the equivalent of pocket editions.

Nicolas **Jenson** (c.1420-1480) was a Frenchman said to have travelled to Mainz in 1458 to acquaint himself with the new invention of printing from cast-metal type. Like Gutenberg himself and many other printers, Jenson was trained in the art of metal working, particularly in the manufacture of gold and silver coins. From this it was a short and logical step to casting metal type. Jenson was in Venice by 1468, in which city he proceeded to print a number of books using roman types of his own design. There are those who consider the roman types of Jenson to be among the finest ever produced. It is certain that his influence on type design was profound and continues to be felt today. Many standard modern type faces can be traced directly back to Jenson.

Claude **Garamond** (fl. 1540's) was another Frenchman but one who lived and worked in France. By his time, the profession of type-designer and punch-cutter was becoming distinct from that of printer and publisher, with the majority of the latter buying in type ready made rather than making their own. Garamond was exclusively a type-designer, manufacturing punches and matrices for general sale. He designed a number of roman types remarkable at once for their beauty and utility. He also designed a set of Greek type for the French king François the First which remained the standard Greek type for the following 200 years. Garamond's name is still in use today to describe a range of founts.

Robert **Granjon** was another sixteenth-century French printer and type designer who sold his type throughout Europe. One of his claims to fame

EPISTOLA PAVLI AD CO-
RINTHIOS PRIMA.

PAVLVS uocatus apostolus Iesu Christi, per uoluntatem dei, & Sosthenes frater, ecclesiæ dei, quæ est Corinthi, sanctificatis per Christum Iesum, uocatis sanctis, unà cum omnibus qui inuocant nomẽ domini nostri Iesu Christi, in quouis loco, uel suo, uel nostro. Gratia uobis & pax à deo patre nostro, & domino Iesu Christo. Gratias ago deo meo semper pro uobis de gratia dei, quæ data est uobis per Christũ Iesum, quod in omnibus ditati estis per ipsum, in omni sermone, & omni cognitione (quibus rebus testimonium Iesu Christi confirmatũ fuit in uobis) adeo, ut nõ destituamini in ullo dono, expectãtes reuelationẽ domini nostri Iesu Christi, q & cõfirmabit uos usq; ad finẽ, inculpatos in die domini nostri Iesu Christi. Fidelis deus, p 1.Thess.5.
quẽ uocati estis ĩ cõsortiũ filij ipsius Iesu Christi domini nostri.

Obsecro autem uos fratres, per nomen domini nostri Iesu Christi, ut idem loquamini omnes, & non sint inter uos dissidia, sed sitis integrum corpus eadem mente, & eadem sententia.

Significatum est enim mihi de uobis fratres mei, à familiaribus Chloæ, quod contentiones sint inter uos. Dico autem illud, quod unusquisq; uestrum dicit: Ego quidem sum Pauli, ego uero Apollo, ego uero Cephæ, ego uero Christi. Num diuisus est Christus? Num Paulus crucifixus est pro uobis? aut in nomine Pauli

R 3 bapti-

Italic type: Froben's edition of Erasmus's "New Testament" (1521)

is the design of a somewhat fantastic type based on an alleged 'gothic' handwriting style. This type is known as **civilité**, after the books in which it was first used (primers of good manners for children). While Granjon's aim of designing an entirely new type to stand alongside roman and italic was not fulfilled, his civilité type was to become the basis for the design of much display type for use in jobbing printing - the printing of advertisements, publicity material and the like. Granjon was also noted for his production of type ornaments, that is, either common letters arranged in decorative patterns or else specially cut patterns.

Christoper **Plantin** (c.1514-1589) was a Frenchman who settled in Antwerp and who conducted business in a large way, with at one time or another printing operations in Paris and Leiden as well as Antwerp itself. Although he designed some types himself Plantin was much more of a publisher with his best work being done using type bought in from other type designers, including Garamond. At its height his printing business in Antwerp was the biggest in Europe and such was his fame he was appointed printer to King Phillip of Spain. It was this appointment that led indirectly to Plantin's greatest typographical achievement, his Polyglot Bible, published between 1568 and 1573.

The important centres of printing on the Continent during the first century and a half of its existence were, successively, Mainz in particular and Germany in general, followed by Venice and then Basle, where Johann **Froben** (1460-1527) was of particular importance. He printed a number of works of Erasmus and also employed Holbein to design title-pages. By the middle of the sixteenth century Paris had gained the ascendancy. In addition to Garamond, mention should be made of the **Estienne** family, one of whom, Robert (1503-1559), was notable as a scholar as well as a printer-publisher. Among many others works, he printed a number of Bibles whose textual content offended the church hierarchy. Eventually Robert quit Paris and established himself at Geneva where he adopted the reformed religion and was free to publish the Bible as he saw fit. His New Testament was the first to divide the text into verses.

The first book printed in English was the work of William **Caxton** (c.1422-1491), though it was printed in the Low Countries and not in England. This book, *The Recuyell of the Histories of Troy*, was the product of Caxton's background as a merchant and diplomat who spent much of his life

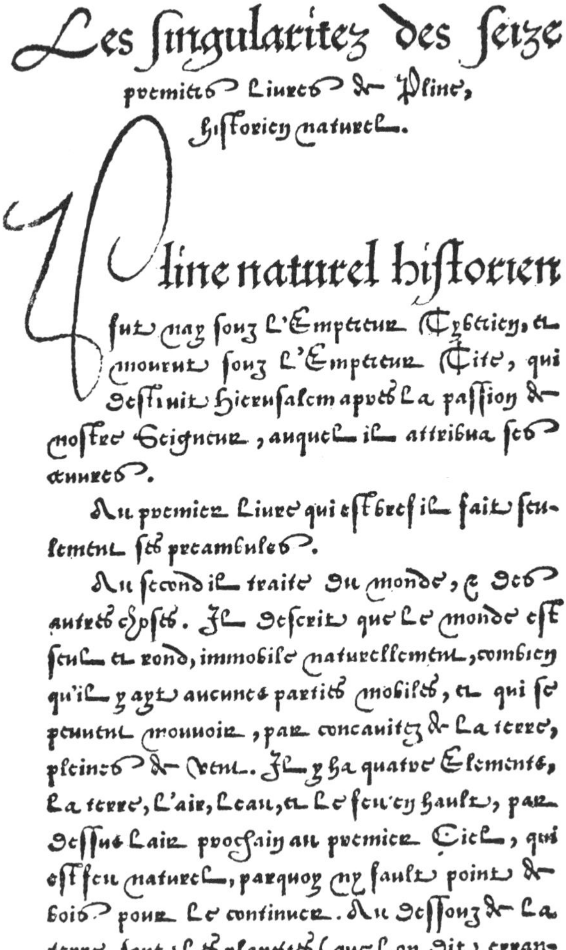

Les singularitez des seize
premiers Livres de Pline,
historien naturel.

Pline naturel historien
fut nay souz l'Empereur Tyberien, et
mourut souz l'Empereur Tite, qui
destruit Hierusalem apres la passion de
nostre Seigneur, auquel il attribua ses
euvres.

Au premier Livre qui est bref il fait seu-
lement ses preambules.

Au second il traite du monde, et des
autres choses. Il descrit que le monde est
seul et rond, immobile naturellement, combien
qu'il y ayt aucunes parties mobiles, et qui se
peuvent mouvoir, par concavitez de la terre,
pleines de vent. Il y ha quatre Elements,
la terre, l'air, l'eau, et le feu en hault, par
dessus l'air prochain au premier Ciel, qui
est feu naturel, parquoy n'y fault point de
bois pour le continuer. Au dessouz de la
terre, sont les planettes (que l'on dit erran-
A ij

Civilité type by Granjon (1539)

on the Continent. The original work was popular at the French court and Caxton undertook an English translation, more for his own amusement than for any other reason. Having familiarised himself with the art of printing while on a visit to Cologne Caxton decided to interest himself in the business when he returned to Bruges. The *Recuyell* was the first book he printed, in 1474. One or two more books were printed at Bruges before Caxton returned to England in 1476 where he set up a printing shop in Westminster. Here he produced the first book printed in England, *The Dictes and Sayings of the Philosophres* in 1477, followed by an edition of *The Canterbury Tales* in 1478. Caxton also printed *The Game of Chess* (1483), a moral tale in which the chess pieces serve as characters. The Low Country influence is very evident in Caxton's printing. Almost all the types he employed were specimens of the gothic, some more readable than others.

Caxton's assistant, **Wynkyn de Worde** (died 1534) took over Caxton's business on the latter's death. While Caxton might be described as a 'gentleman publisher', a literary man who took as much interest in the matter he was printing as the mechanics of the business, Wynkyn de Worde was primarily a businessman-printer producing popular editions of the classics and current literature as well as school text books in large numbers. Although he did design a type of his own, he also used the types left to him by Caxton as well as the wood blocks for illustrations. Indeed, he would use the same block many times in different books over the years.

While the sixteenth century saw much fine printing being done at many centres on the Continent English printing of the same period was confined almost entirely to journeyman work. This may be explained partly by the fact that England was outside the main intellectual currents of the time, not quite a backward island but certainly 'off-shore'. The market for printed books must have been small; there was little incentive for the printer to interest himself in anything other than basic printing at an economic cost. Type was as often as not bought in from northern Europe, thus the indigenous type-founding industry was for long a rudimentary affair.

Two exceptions worth mentioning are first of all Richard Pynson (d. 1530) and, later in the century, John Day (1522-1584) who, after some vicissitudes, established himself as the main printer of the Elizabethan period. He had cut a set of roman and italic faces in the 1570's which he used to great effect.

The fourth tractate and the last of the progressyon and draughtes of the forsayd playe of the chesse

The first chapitre of the fourth tractate of the chesse borde in generall how it is maad capitulo primo

E haue deuysed aboue the thynges that apperteyne W, Unto the formes of the chesse men and of their offices. that is to wete as wel of noble men as of the comyn peple / Than hit aperteyneth that we sholde deuyse shortly how they yssue and goon out of the places where they be sette . And first we ought to speke of the forme and of the facion of the chequer after that hit representeth and

A page from J. de Cessoli's "Game of Chess", with wood-cut illustration, printed by Caxton about 1483

During the first half of the century, in particular, such was the rudimentary state of English printing that many books for the English market were actually printed abroad and imported into this country. Reasons other than economic probably accounted for the fact that the first complete Bible in English was also printed abroad, in Antwerp in 1535. Henry VIII was for a time violently opposed to the idea of a vernacular translation of the scriptures. Tyndale, the translator, was murdered by Henry's agents in 1536, though Henry's political vacillations were such that within two or three years of Tyndale's death copies of his English Bible were being printed in England by the king's own printer.

By the middle of the century, matters had begun to change somewhat, a change marked by the incorporation of the Worshipful **Company of Stationers**. This guild had been founded in the early fifteenth century, before the introduction of the printing press. By the 1550's it was felt that too many people were turning to printing for a livelihood and that some control was necessary. In 1557 the company was granted a charter which gave it an effective veto over who could set up in business as a printer - an early form of closed shop. Additionally, all publications had to be registered with the Company, and sometimes the publisher would state in his book that the work had been licensed by the Company.

In Holland, the firm of **Elzevir** was founded in Amsterdam in 1638 and continued in existence until well into the eighteenth century. The Elzevirs were, interestingly, among the first of a new and modern breed - printers rather than scholars, a distinction which we today take for granted but which in the early days of printing was by no means clear-cut. The Elzevirs were interested in the competent printing of books that would sell; matters of scholarship, of authorship, of editorial control were not their concern but that of the author or editor. The majority of their books were printed in small formats, and some eighty percent consisted of Latin texts, doubtless supplying the educational establishments of the day. Booksellers today will still draw attention to the fact that a certain book is an Elzevir printing, though it isn't always obvious that this is a selling point given the journeyman nature of much of their later work.

The seventeenth century was a period of relative decline as far as developments in printing were concerned; the age of the great Continental scholar-printers was past, and like their counterparts in England, printers in

Tercia etas mũdi Foliũ XXXIIII

Linea regũ assiriorum

Ascades.

Amyntbas

Bellothus

Aptheros Eructoni⁹ Fenix Cadmus

Aptheros Rex crethe primo mellis colligendi vsum inuenit. hui⁹ nata ex incestu concepit de qua mirabilia narrãt. Et post ibidẽ fili⁹ regnauit z dictus fuit auidis legesq fecit et prim⁹ boues aratro iunxit. Ericonius Athenensiũ priceps prim⁹ in grecia quadrigã excogitauit. Fenix ille in tyro et sydone regnauit vsuq litterarũ tradidit. z colores feniceos quo capitalia fierent inuenit. A B Γ Δ Alpha vita Gãma Delta.

Corinth⁹ vrbs fuit Achaie olim insignis qui primũ a Sysipho latrone Acoli sup Ischmõ i medio maris ionij z egei cõstructa fuit. Octuagesimo etatis moysi ãno. Primo Certhyra deiñ aucta Ephyra vocata. Vñ z apud virgiliũ Ephyreaq era. Nã Corinthij in ere fundẽdo pricipatũ obtinebãt Eo q ibi pulcherria z artificiosa eiusmodi eris fiebãt vasa. Sz p⁹ h euersa z ab Corintho Orestis filio istaurata Corinth⁹ cognoiata fuit. Ultio a romanis accensa nũq coaluit vt oñdit flor⁹ z iustin⁹. Fuitq teste Apulegio libro de magica regionis caput. Apud corinthios pmũ imperiũ assumpsit z regnuit Aletes grecus luctator victoriosissim⁹. Regnatũq ẽ in Corintho sb regib⁹ duodeci. annis 323. Postea respublica p annuos magistrat⁹ gubernari cepta est. Poloponesus puicia quã hodie latini Moreã vocãt toti⁹ grecie quondã arx dicta regio ẽ pene insula. haud vlli terre nobilitate p⁹ ferẽda. Inter duo maria Egeũ z Ionũ. platani folio similis. Angustia vñ pcedit Ischmos appellat. in ea strictura q Cherroneson efficit ciuitas ẽ chorintbi. medio interuallo colli applicata. Sz has ipas angustias (vt plini⁹ retulit) pfodere nauigabili alueo tentauere Demetri⁹ rex Cesar dictator cay⁹ princeps. domici⁹ nero infausto (vt oĩ exitu patuit) incepto Grecie pncipes postq Turcoz potẽtia europã penetrauit ex mari ad mare pducto p angustias muro peloponesiis a reliq grecia disiũxerũt Murũ examiliũ vocauere Corintheos ab idoloz cultura ad verã dei religionẽ Paul⁹ aplus ratioib⁹ z doctrina atq miraclis ptraxit. Nũc ea regio tota impio Turcoz adiecta est.

Corinthus

A page from Anton Koberger's "Nuremberg Chronicle", 1493

Germany, France, Italy and elsewhere seemed preoccupied with the day to day business of making a living through their work. The reasons for this are many and varied. Political and social upheaval undoubtedly played its part; and in the seventeenth century in England attempts by government to control the activities of the press and all to do with it must have discouraged many printers from experimenting. More generally it is fair to postulate that the first great wave of artistic endeavour set in motion by the new invention had simply run its course and died a natural death, exhausted. It wasn't until the eighteenth century that printers took up the challenge again, bringing new thought to printing techniques and type design. In England, in particular, the eighteenth century witnessed the first important indigenous work in what by then was being called 'typography'.

The proximate cause of this revival of interest was Dutch type-founding. The Dutch had been active in the field almost continuously since the beginnings of printing itself. While much of their work in the seventeenth century was of no great merit, one or two type designers stood out above the rest. The type-founding firm of **Enschedé** was established in Haarlem in 1703. Towards the end of the seventeenth century a certain Bishop Fell imported into England from Holland a set of punches and matrices to produce type for the use of the university press at Oxford. This type became known as the **Fell** fount and derivations of it were in use by the Oxford University Press until quite recently.

Dutch type-founding was also the inspiration for the work of one of the most important English type designers, William **Caslon** (1692-1766). He first began designing types in the 1720's, in imitation of some Dutch types then in use in England. It wasn't long before he was cutting types to his own design, the first of which, a 12-point roman fount, appeared in 1725. Caslon's reputation has undergone something of a revision in the last few decades, with suggestions that not all of his founts are of equal worth. Whatever the merits of this argument, it is undeniable that Caslon had a profound influence on English type design, with founts bearing his name still in use today.

The second important figure in eighteenth century English typography was John **Baskerville** (1706-1775). He came to printing rather late in life, once he had made his fortune elsewhere, and from the very beginning was concerned to produce books of the finest quality possible. This entailed a complete rethinking of all aspects of book production, in particular, the manufacture of paper and ink, and the design of type. Such was his search for perfection that it took him seven years to produce his first book, an edition of Virgil, published in 1757. Baskerville was a 'gentleman-amateur', not interested in producing books for profit but 'such only, as are *books* of *Consequence*, of *intrinsic merit*, or *established Reputation*, and which the public may be pleased to see in an elegant dress, and to purchase at such a price, as will repay the extraordinary care and expence that must necessarily be bestowed upon them...' Baskerville's 'elegant dress' relied for its effect upon an almost severely plain appearance - type cast to his own austere design, carefully set and more widely spaced than was usual and with an almost complete lack of ornament. One of Baskerville's innovations involved pressing the printed sheet between plates of heated copper to give the print a burnished appearance.

France in the eighteenth century witnessed a similar revival of interest in fine printing, with Louis XIV commissioning in 1692 a completely new series of types for the exclusive use of the Royal Printing Office. As with so many aspects of French cultural life, the design was the responsibility of a committee, with the punch cutter merely being told to work to the designs presented. Nevertheless, the first and most famous 'royal' punch cutter, Philippe **Grandjean** (1666-1714), managed to impose something of his personality on the design, and the first founts from this venture came to be identified with his name.

The family of **Fournier** were of great importance in the history of French type design through several generations. One of the earliest of the family, Jean Pierre Fournier (1706-1783) owned a type-foundry which included in its stock many old punches and matrices of the great printers of the past, notably Garamond. Another of the family, and brother of Jean Pierre, was Pierre Simon Fournier (1712-1768), who, as well being responsible for much fine printing, made the first attempt to standardize sizes of type using the point system described above. In contrast to Baskerville, the Fourniers collectively placed great emphasis on ornamentation, almost as much as on the design of the type itself, with the result that their title-pages in particular are resplendent with decorative effects.

Didot is another important name in the history of French typography. The first of the family to become involved in printing was born in 1689 and his descendants were still active some 200 years later. As well as designing type for their own printing, the Didot family seemed to have been as interested in the technical side of printing. Collectively they were responsible for introducing Baskerville's paper-making techniques into France, for improving upon and fixing the point system of measurement invented by Fournier, for the invention of a method for the mechanical casting of type and for the invention of the stereotype plate (a method of printing from a single block of type metal).

Baskerville also plays a part in French typography. His work was appreciated as much on the Continent as it was in England, indeed perhaps more so, at least in the years immediately following his death, when much of his equipment and type was exported to France. There it was used, among other things, to print the first copies of the official newspaper of the Revolution, a use which would probably have a brought a frown to the brow of the somewhat conservative Baskerville.

Finally, I should mention one Italian printer of the late eighteenth century, Giambattista **Bodoni** (1740-1813). Bodoni had his early education at the hands of his father, also a printer, and then went to work at Rome, where he developed an interest in non-roman alphabets. On his return to his native city of Parma, he began printing by using type from other type designers, particularly those of the Fournier family. However, by the end of the eighteenth century he had designed a number of 'modern' founts - modern in the sense that they prefigure much typographical work of the later nineteenth century - and it is for these that he is chiefly remembered.

The stated purpose of this chapter was to introduce some of the most important figures in the early history of printing. This has entailed an undue concentration on what for want of a better term may be described as 'fine printing'. It is perhaps worth recalling that the work of the printers discussed represents, in general terms, only the highest standard of printing, the exception rather than the rule. There were, besides these printers, many thousands of others at work everywhere and at all times, producing for the most part quite ordinary books, undistinguished in any way at all. There were, as well, printers producing sometimes quite dreadful specimens of the art.

To end this survey at the opening of the nineteenth century is not entirely arbitrary, as I suggested at the beginning of the chapter. The progressive mechanisation of all aspects of the printing process had profound effects; the book became far more a simple object of utility - something to be read - rather than an object upon which artist-craftsmen could exercise their skill. The roles of printer and publisher rapidly became quite distinct. The publisher became the driving force (whose main concern was to ensure a return on his investment), commissioning the book and instructing the printer as to type and paper. The manufacture of type developed into a further, separate activity, with the printer progressively more likely to buy in type ready-made, selecting from a standard well-known range, rather than commission a design himself. It is arguable that fine printing is only possible when all these functions are brought together under one roof, or head, and this is precisely what occurred late in the nineteenth century, with the rise of the private press.

Paper

For the person with a general interest in books, a basic knowledge of the history of paper and its methods of manufacture is perhaps not essential, but is certainly useful to an understanding of the book as a whole. It is of most use when dealing with books printed before about 1800, that is, before the introduction of machine-made paper. In the case of very early books, in particular, a study of the paper the book is printed on will often, in the absence of other evidence, identify not only the time of printing but the place as well, occasionally even the printer. In this chapter I shall concentrate almost exclusively on the hand-made product, that is paper produced up to the beginning of the nineteenth century.

History

As with so much else in the field of printing, the earliest records of paper-making are to be found in China. From the second or third centuries A.D. various types of cloth and bark were used to produce a material which probably bore more resemblance to felt than to our idea of paper, but which nevertheless was used for writing, and later for printing. The reports of early European travellers such as Marco Polo bear witness to this invention.

As the knowledge of paper-making travelled westwards, often by conquest, the Arabs were quick to perceive the advantages of paper over papyrus, not least because they already cultivated flax in great quantities and this crop made an ideal raw material. By the end of the eighth century A.D. paper-mills had been established at several sites in the Middle East, including Baghdad, while by the end of the twelfth century some 400 mills are recorded in Morocco at Fez.

While paper had been imported into Europe through such ports as Venice from an early date, its actual manufacture in Europe did not begin until the twelfth or thirteenth century. Again, the introduction was the result of conquest, this time the Arabs' conquest of Spain. As they settled in Spain, the Arabs brought with them an entire civilisation, which included the art of paper-making. From Spain, knowledge of the process spread slowly into the rest of Europe, with the first recorded paper-mill outside Spain being established in Italy about 1268. The slow spread of paper-making was due partly to a prejudice in favour of **parchment**. Parchment is the inner skin of a hide which has been split. Its durability and smooth surface made it the ideal material, among other things, for the production of illuminated manuscripts. But parchment was also used for more mundane purposes and the authorities, suspicious of the new-fangled substance, often sought to enforce the use of parchment. It was not until the invention of printing that paper came into its own. The new invention created a huge demand for material on which to print; only paper could be manufactured in sufficient quantity to satisfy that demand.

Materials

Almost any fibrous material can be used as the raw material for paper. Some 2,000 different substances have been identified as having been used at one time or another. The Chinese initially used silk rags, turning later to hemp and flax. Bark from the mulberry tree was also used. The Arabs also used hemp, though not raw hemp. Instead they recycled hemp that had already been exploited in some other fashion, such as ropes, as a result of which the fibres had already been degraded to an extent.

Hemp was also the preferred material of the early European paper-makers, together with linen rags and canvas. With the demand for paper increasing exponentially through the fifteenth and sixteenth centuries, the authorities often had to enact laws to regulate the collection of old rags, such was the money to be made out of the business of supplying paper mills. And it was economic necessity which stimulated the search for substitute raw materials, as the supply of rags failed to match the demand for paper. In the eighteenth century experiments were conducted with various outlandish materials (wasps's nests, mosses, cabbage-stalks, nettles, saw-dust); by the beginning of the nineteenth, straw and wood had emerged as the favourites, while in 1857 esparto grass was first used. Unfortunately, the paper produced from these new raw materials was, and is, often of a distinctly poorer quality than that produced from rags, which is why the paper of eighteenth-century books and earlier often appears fresher and more wholesome than that of books of quite recent date. Rags are still occasionally used today to produce the highest quality paper, which is known as **rag paper**.

Processes

The essential process in the manufacture of paper is the reduction of the raw material to its original fibres. The Chinese thought it necessary to first 'rot' the material by prolonged and repeated immersion in water. The fermentation which ensued destroyed everything but the fibres. This initial processing was also followed by European paper-makers until early in the nineteenth century. The Arabs used a number of different chemical additives such as lime to produce the same result.

The next stage of the process consists in breaking the fibres to produce a pulp. This is done by a variety of means. In the earliest days, mortar and pestle, flails and human feet were all employed. The mills of Fez were largely driven by water power, and water was used to drive some of the earliest mills in Europe, with the pulp being ground between mill- stones. In the eighteenth century steam was employed to drive a series of beaters.

The end product of this process of beating and stamping is a thin pulp in which the broken fibres are held in a watery solution. When the pulp is of the right consistency, a mould is dipped into the vat and a quantity of pulp scooped up. The 'mould' is in fact no more than a screen or mesh of wires upon which the pulp is levelled into the shape and thickness of the final sheet of paper. The gaps in the mesh allow the excess water to drain off rapidly. All the skill of the paper-maker is concentrated in the ability to 'level' the pulp in the mould in a single movement of the arms, to produce a smooth sheet of even consistency and without blemishes.

The use of wire screens gives rise to the typical appearance of hand-made European paper when held up to the light: firstly, there is a series of lines running in one direction and closely packed together (**laid lines**); secondly, running at right angles to the laid lines is a second set of lines set quite far apart (**chain lines**). This pattern is merely the design of the wire screen unavoidably impressed into the paper in the initial drying. Paper which displays these lines is called **laid paper**, though the term is not synonymous with hand-made paper, since machine-made papers sometimes have lines impressed into them in imitation of the hand-made product.

Once the excess water had drained off, the sheet would be turned out of the mould onto a piece of felt with a second piece of felt placed over it. A second sheet of paper would then be turned out onto the second piece of felt, and this in turn covered with felt. After a number of semi-dried sheets had been built into a pile in this manner they would be put into a screw press and more water squeezed out.

If the paper is to take the ink - if it is to be anything more than blotting paper - it must be **sized**. Sizing consists, very simply, in the addition, either to the pulp or to the semi-dried sheet, of a glue or gelatine. The Arabs and Chinese were apparently in the habit of adding size to the pulp itself, while European manufacturers preferred treating the semi-dried sheet. The size was made by boiling and reducing animal skins. After being dipped individually into the bath of size, a quantity of sheets would be stacked together and put into the press and the excess size squeezed out. The single sheets would then be peeled off and hung up to dry.

Wove paper is paper manufactured using a mould in which the wires have been woven so close together in a manner so fine as to leave no impression in the finished paper corresponding to laid lines and chain lines. The Birmingham printer, John Baskerville, is credited with the invention of wove paper. As I mentioned in the preceding chapter, his interest was in producing fine editions and he found existing papers too coarse for his purposes. Baskerville invented the new technique around the middle of the eighteenth century but it was not until the early nineteenth century that it came into general use with its adaptation to a mechanically-driven continuous web which began to replace the traditional mould. From then on, almost all paper used in ordinary books was of the wove sort. The first manufacturers of wove paper often described it as 'vellum' as a tribute to its smooth and glossy surface, not unlike vellum proper (animal skin). Even today a few books are printed on paper described as **Japanese vellum**. In French it is known as **vélin**.

Given the method of manufacture of hand-made paper, the edges of the sheet are inevitably rather rough. In most cases, when the book is bound, these rough edges would be trimmed clean. Occasionally, the binder would leave them untrimmed, through laziness, forgetfulness or sometimes intentionally,

An early European paper-mill showing: a water-wheel driving beaters; the paper-maker holding a mould over the vat of pulp; an assistant operating a screw press; sheets hung up for drying.

to impart an 'antiquarian feel' to the book. When the leaves are untrimmed the book is described as **uncut**. ('Uncut' is not to be confused with **unopened**, which means that the folds of the sheets have not been slit open.)

These rough untrimmed edges of the paper are sometimes known as **deckle edges**, after the deckle, the frame of the mould in which the paper is made. Many booksellers restrict the use of the term 'deckle edge' to books of the late nineteenth or twentieth centuries, with the implication that the printer and publisher intended the rough edges to be an integral part of the finished book.

Mould-made paper represents an attempt to combine the advantages of machinery with the perceived superiority of hand-made paper. It involves recreating the appearance of hand-made paper - in particular the laid lines and chain lines - by mechanical means. Needless to say, mould-made papers date only from the advent of machine-made paper and are most commonly found in fine editions of the last hundred years or so.

Cheap papers of the nineteenth and twentieth centuries are often of such poor quality that they become discoloured after only a few years. Perhaps the worst paper used for printing in modern times is to be found in French paperbacks. Not only does the paper turn an unpleasant brown, it also becomes very friable, breaking up as the book is handled. Some papers used in the fifteenth century, by contrast, are still as clean and fresh today as when they were first produced.

As well as liking a good quality paper collectors have always had a prejudice in favour of large quantities of it. This prejudice is satisfied by books with **wide margins** , that is, books with a small amount of text on each page relative to the size of the leaf. A common term for this kind of book is **large paper copy**.

Although the bulk of paper today is machine-made, there are still manufacturers producing paper by hand, usually in small workshops, using a variety of materials and techniques. Their products are often destined for use by the innumerable private presses which have flourished since the war.

Watermarks

The term **watermark** refers to any impression left in the body of the paper during the process of manufacture. Thus the laid lines and chain lines are a form of watermark. Strictly, though, the term is now reserved for those impressions which have been made deliberately, with the intention of conveying information. Though a variety of methods have been employed to produce watermarks, the simplest and most common involves attaching to the mould - itself a wire mesh - a design also constructed out of wire. As with the lines, this design or motif can be seen when the paper is held up to the light.

The subject of watermarks constitutes a whole field of study in itself. The first watermark has been dated to around 1282 and some 16,000 different watermarks have been identified in papers produced before the beginning of the seventeenth century. And there is a bewildering variety of designs. Paper-makers drew their inspiration from heraldry, religion, anatomy and dress, as well as many other areas. Watermarks were used for several different purposes: to identify the paper-maker, to date the paper and to indicate its quality. Perhaps most importantly, some watermarks came to be used to mark the size of the sheet of paper.

A variety of different sizes of sheet were manufactured by the process described above. From the earliest times, each country showed a tendency to standardization of sheet sizes. One of the major forces for standardization was the dimensions of the printing press itself. The printing press represented a large investment in money, and could be expected to be in use for many years. The construction of presses was confined to a relatively small number of manufacturers, who naturally concentrated on producing standard-sized models. Thus the paper-makers were obliged, for commercial reasons, to produce sizes of sheet to fit the various sizes of press. By the eighteenth century, standardization of sheet size had reached the point where it was subject to government regulation in some Continental countries. Not only were the sizes of sheet determined by law, but also the various watermarks which were used to identify those different sizes.

Some of the more common watermarks used to indicate size of sheet are as follows:

Foolscap: (a 'fool's cap', ie., the cap of a jester or Punch figure): 17 x 13.25 inches

Crown: 15 x 20 inches

Demy: (represented by a fleur-de-lis within a shield): 22.5 x 17.5 inches

Royal: (a fleur-de-lis above a shield): 20 x 25 inches

Elephant: 28 x 23 inches.

Why should the book collector be interested in sizes of paper and watermarks? Apart from any intrinsic interest, the size of the sheet is one determinant of the overall size and shape of the finished book, and this is of the first importance to the bibliographer. Some booksellers and cataloguers still use the names of the various watermarks in their descriptions of books.

The Printed Sheet

The basic unit of the book is the single printed sheet. Most books are built up from a number of printed sheets folded then sewn together. Once the sheets have been folded and sewn, the edges are trimmed, thereby cutting open the folds. (A small number of books of the nineteenth century, as well as many modern paperbacks, have their individual leaves glued together, without sewing. This type of construction will be dealt with later.)

For an understanding of how the book is made up, the first thing to consider is the individual sheet. The first, basic, fact to grasp is that the sheet produced by the printer does not correspond to the printed leaf as it appears in the book.

The **leaf** has two pages, one on the front and one on the back. For some bibliographical purposes the 'front' of the leaf is described as the **recto** and the back of the leaf as the **verso**. The recto of the leaf is the side first exposed, on the right-hand side of the opened book. Facing it, on the left-hand side, is the verso of the preceding leaf. Each leaf, obviously, has both a recto and a verso. 'Recto' and 'verso' are frequently abbreviated in catalogues and the like to 'r' and 'v'.

What is involved in the printing of a sheet can best be understood through a simple exercise. Take a sheet of A4 paper and fold it once down the centre (ie., so that the fold runs parallel to the shorter sides of the sheet). You now have the equivalent of two leaves (or four pages), and what you have produced is an example of a **folio** format. A book in folio format would consist of a number of printed sheets folded in the manner described and sewn together. The **format** of the book may be defined as a function of the number of times the sheet has been folded.

Take another sheet of A4, fold it once as for folio, then fold it a second time, so that the second fold runs at right angles to the first (and the second fold runs parallel to the shorter sides). You now have an example of a **quarto** format. A sheet which is in quarto format has four leaves (or eight pages), and if the same size sheet was used as for the folio, then each leaf will be half the size of the folio leaf. In a quarto folding, the two pairs of leaves will be joined at the top. Once the folded sheets have been sewn together, and before the binding is put on, the top edges will be trimmed with a guillotine to open the leaves.

Probably the most common format is **octavo**, which is the next size down from quarto, ie., a sheet folded three times to produce eight leaves (or sixteen pages). In an octavo folding all four pairs of leaves would be joined at their top edges and the second of the pairs along their outer edges.

Folio, quarto and octavo are the three most common formats for books. Many booksellers abbreviate 'quarto' to **4to** and 'octavo' to **8vo**. Some booksellers, but by no means all, abbreviate 'folio' to **2o**.

Less common formats are as follows:

Duodecimo, usually written and spoken '12mo' (**twelve-mo**)

Sextodecimo, almost always written and spoken '16mo' (**sixteen-mo**)

Vicesimo-quarto, near universally written and spoken '24mo' (**twentyfour-mo**)

Tricesimo-secundo, near universally written and spoken '32mo' (**thirtytwo-mo**).

These are the standard terms that booksellers and auctioneers use when describing the format of books.

The same principles of folding apply with the smaller formats. However, while the foldings for 16mo and 32mo present no theoretical problem, being simple extensions of the sequence 2o, 4to, 8vo, the foldings for 12mo and 24mo are slighty different and somewhat eccentric. A little more will be said about these formats in the next chapter. A further possible format is 18mo, though this is so rare, at least, in English books that it can safely be ignored.

At this point I need to introduce another technical term, the **gathering**. 'Gathering' describes the printed sheet once it has been folded and sewn. In the examples considered so far, the gathering would correspond to a single folded sheet. However, the gathering is defined not only by the sheet but also by the sewing. In the following chapter we shall look at cases of two or more sheets folded and sewn together as one. In these cases the two sheets - or however many - would constitute a single gathering.

A synonym for 'gathering' sometimes met with is **quire**. This bibliographer's sense of the word must be distinguished from the paper manufacturer's use of the same word to mean a part of a ream.

The final size and shape of the book depend not only on the number of times the sheet has been folded (format) but also on the size of the original sheet. In the chapter on paper we saw how different watermarks were used to indicate different dimensions of paper. If the bookseller wants to give the fullest possible information in his catalogue then rather than limiting himself to the description, for example, '8vo', he will identify the size of the original sheet by adding the relevant watermark, for example, 'Crown 8vo', 'Royal 8vo', 'Demy 8vo'. Thus the person reading the catalogue can deduce almost the exact size of the leaf, always allowing a margin for what the binder may have trimmed off.

It has to be said that many booksellers are not as exact as this in their descriptions. If they decide to give any information at all in addition to the bare format they will often employ one of a series of more or less imprecise qualifying adjectives, as in 'tall 8vo', 'small 8vo', 'large quarto', 'oblong 4to'.

Finally, I should mention the **broadsheet**, which, while technically a format like quarto or octavo, in practice bears little relation to what we have been considering. A bibliographical expression for this format, though not one universally acknowledged, is **1o**. Now, as the simplest format we have met with to date is folio (2o), which is a sheet folded once only, the nimble-minded may have already deduced that '1o' can only mean a sheet that has not been folded at all, and they would be correct. A broadsheet is a single printed sheet of paper, not folded. A purist might insist that to qualify as a broadsheet, the sheet must be printed on one side of the paper only, though the term is commonly used for a sheet printed on both sides. The purist might further insist that the term can only be applied to a sheet whose dimensions correspond to one of the standard sizes (crown, royal, etc.) in other words, not to a piece of paper cut from such a sheet. 'Broadsheet' is sometimes abbreviated to **b.s.**

Imposition

In the preceding chapter we saw how the individual sheets are folded to produce the pages of the book. We also should consider briefly how the sheet itself is printed. The printer's technical term to describe the process of setting up the blocks of type for each sheet is called **imposition**.

Imposition is not a matter of the first importance to the majority of collectors (and, be it said, booksellers). Many such no doubt pass their entire lives without coming up against the subject. But it is important to at least know what it is and to have a passing acquaintance with the principles involved. And for anyone whose interest is in very old books imposition is an essential study, since it often reveals significant information about the book's manufacture and make-up.

Imposition is a relatively complicated matter since each sheet will have printed on it a number of pages. A book that is to be of folio format will have four pages printed on each sheet (two on each side); a sheet for a quarto format will have eight pages (four to each side).

Taking a folio format as our example, the printer's task is to set up four separate pages of type in two pairs. Each pair of page-type is locked in a chase. Each pair of chases arranged to print the whole of one side of a sheet is known as a **forme**. For the printing of a sheet, two formes will be necessary (corresponding to the two sides of the sheet). They are known as the 'outer' forme and the 'inner' forme.

Figure 1 shows how the two formes are set up for the printing of a folio.

Folio imposition is relatively simple. Quarto imposition is a little more complicated, since the printer is printing eight pages simultaneously.

Octavo imposition is more complicated still (figure 2).

What we have looked at so far represents what might be termed 'standard' imposition. There are a number of variations upon this standard method, some of which are met with quite often and which are therefore worth noting.

The most common of these variations involves the doubling, or even trebling, of the number of sheets which are put together in a single gathering. In the case of folio volumes, particularly, two or three separate sheets may be combined into one gathering. If two folio sheets are combined, one would be inserted inside the other, and the two held together with a single sewing through their centre folds. It follows that the imposition in this case must be different from that of an ordinary folio sheet. The gathering will contain four leaves, instead of the usual two. The 'outer' sheet will bear the page numbers 1 and 2, and 7 and 8, the 'inner' sheet will bear the page numbers 3 and 4, and 5 and 6.

A book of this construction would be described as 'folio in fours', ie., a folio volume with four leaves to each gathering. Also quite common is 'folio in sixes', ie., three folio sheets combined in a single gathering, giving six leaves.

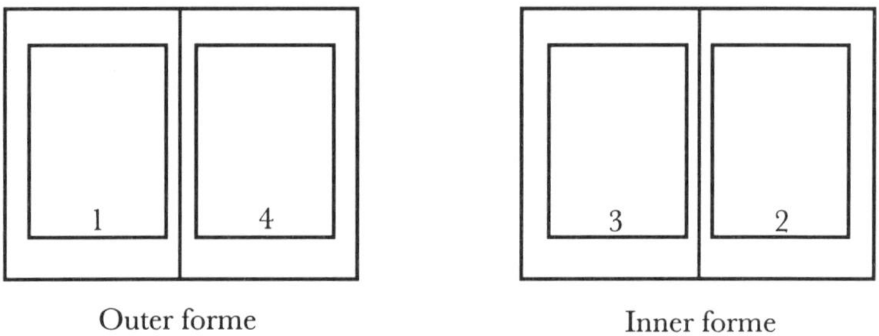

Figure 1. Type-pages imposed for a sheet in folio

Figure 2. Type-pages imposed for a sheet in octavo

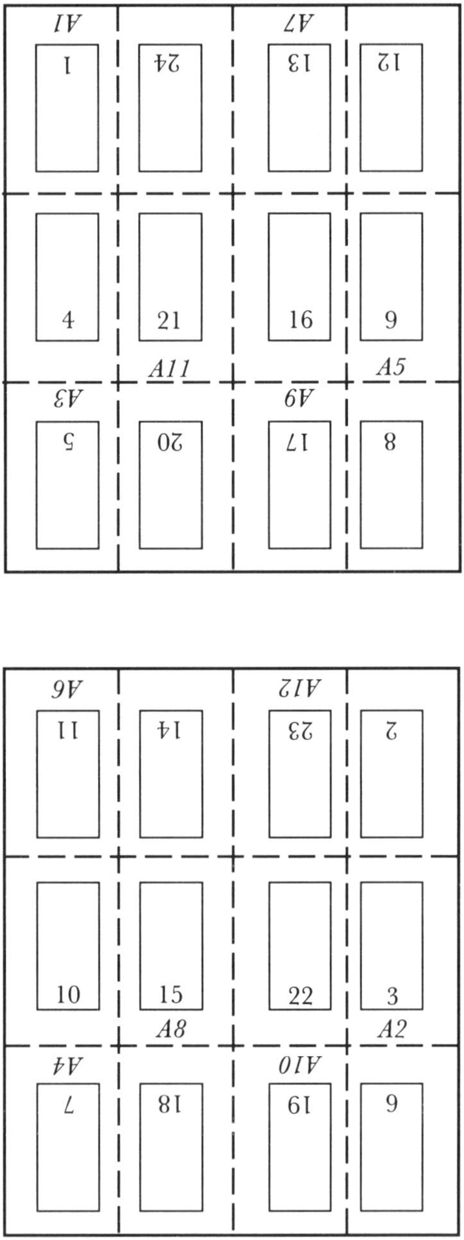

Figure 3. A sheet printed in twelve-mo, ready for folding

There are several reasons why a book should be printed as folio in fours or sixes. The most important has to do with the saving of time and effort in the sewing. A folio in sixes requires only one third of the sewing which would be entailed in the production of an ordinary folio book with the same number of leaves. A second, related, reason concerns the binding of the book. A large amount of sewing tends to to make the back of the book unduly bulky; the binder therefore has a difficult job to produce an acceptable binding.

The same principle of combining two sheets in one gathering is met with occasionally in other formats. You might for example, come across a 'quarto in eights'.

In the previous chapter it was noted that the folding of the smaller formats, in particular, 12mo and 24mo, could be rather complicated. This is a consequence of the complexities of 12mo and 24mo imposition. There are several alternative ways of imposing a sheet for 12mo or 24mo. Of the two formats, 12mo is the one most commonly encountered. An example of a 12mo imposition popular in the nineteenth century is given in figure 3. To understand how the sheet is divided up, you may like to undertake another exercise in paper folding. The sheet is first folded into equal thirds, with each fold running parallel to the shorter sides of the sheet; the sheet is then folded in half, still with the fold running parallel to the shorter side, and folded once more, with this final fold running parallel to the immediately previous fold. If all this sounds rather complicated, it is because 12mo imposition is complicated! If you have folded the paper correctly, when opened up again it should have crease lines corresponding to the broken lines in figure 3.

Signatures

We have studied the way in which the sheet is printed and folded to produce a series of consecutive pages. If you attempted the suggested exercises - folding a sheet of paper to imitate the various formats, 4to, 8vo, &c - you may have realised how awkward it would be to check using the page numbers whether the pages are in the correct sequence, not least because some of the pages are joined at either the top or outer edge. Checking is done by means of the signature.

The **signature** is a letter of the alphabet - or, in modern books, sometimes a numeral - which is printed at the foot of the first page of each gathering (or the recto of the first leaf of each gathering) by the printer as an aid to the binder. Consecutive gatherings bear consecutive letters - A,B,C,&c - thus allowing the binder to see at a glance that he has all the gatherings in the correct order before he begins to sew them together.

But the signature is also used to help the binder fold each individual sheet correctly. The recto of the first leaf (page 1) is signed, say 'A'; the recto of the second leaf (page 3) is signed 'A2' (or, using roman numerals, 'Aii'); the recto of the third leaf (page 5) is signed 'A3' (or 'Aiii'), and so on. In this way the binder has a quick and easy guide to tell him that the sheet has been folded correctly.

A standard quarto book might have the leaves signed as follows: A at the foot of page 1 and Aii at the foot of page 3. With a quarto format it is usual to sign only the first two leaves of each gathering - if the first two leaves are in the correct order then the sheet must have been folded correctly.

A standard octavo book might be signed as follows: A (page 1), Aii (page 3), Aiii (page 5), Aiv (page 7), Av (page 9). With more modern books in octavo format, however, it is not uncommon to find only the first two leaves signed.

The signature had its origin in manuscript production, before the invention of printing. Scribes were in the habit of marking the foot of each page with a letter to indicate to the binder the order in which the leaves should be bound. The first printers not unnaturally took over the practice, and indeed, the first signatures in printed books were often written in by hand on the printed sheet. Thus signatures have been in existence since the very earliest days of printing. It is hardly surprising, therefore, that over the centuries, in different countries and with different printers, practice should vary considerably, giving rise to numerous interesting problems of interpretation and understanding for the present-day bibliographer.

The importance of the signature to us now is that it allows us to identify the format of the book. (One of the interests of the bibliographer, faced with a book many years old, is to try to determine its format, in other words, to work back from the finished book in front of him to the sheets which the printer actually produced and which the binder folded and sewed.) Regardless of any peculiarities of signing *within* each gathering, in most cases the number of leaves between each different signature letter will indicate the format of the book. If a book has eight leaves between signature letters A and B it is almost certainly an octavo format. Four leaves between A and B (or G and H, or P and Q) will suggest a quarto format; twelve leaves, a duodecimo format. (With 12mo formats, the signature letters sometimes change after 6 leaves instead of twelve. This has to do with the complications of 12mo imposition already touched on. Even in such cases, though, the format is virtually certain to be 12mo since firstly, '6mo' is a mere theoretical possibility, and secondly, only the formats 12mo and 24mo are divisible by 6 (disregarding 18mo). And general dimensions alone will distinguish a 12mo from a 24mo, the former being roughly the size of a small 8vo, while the latter verges on the miniature.)

Some particular aspects of the signature need to be mentioned. The printer worked through the alphabet with his signatures - A,B,C,D,&c. The printer's alphabet was the Latin, or early Roman alphabet, which consisted of 23 letters, not 26. The letters J,U and W did not appear. Even when these letters began to be introduced into the general alphabet in the sixteenth century, and as a consequence began to figure in printers' founts, the alphabet of signatures remained at 23 letters.

Twenty-three signature letters for a quarto book would allow only 184 pages (23 x 4 = 92 leaves x 2 = 184 pages). What happened when the printer got to Z? The obvious thing to do would be to start again at the beginning, and this is what he did. But to avoid confusion, he doubled the number of letters, AA, AA2, AA3, and so on. Sometimes the printer would use a small letter, Aa, Aaii, Aaiii, &c. It isn't uncommon in early books to find signing stretching to Aaa or even Aaaa!

A further point relates to the preliminary leaves, or all those pages that appear before the text proper of the book. It was customary, and indeed still is, to print these pages last, after the text of the book. The printer would often set aside the letter A for the signing of these preliminary leaves and begin the signing of the text of the book with the letter B. The practice of signing the preliminary leaves varied considerably; very often they weren't signed at all. So if you cannot find a signature letter A in a book this doesn't generally mean that something is missing.

With very old books in particular, sixteenth century or earlier, the printer may have utilised some quite arbitrary sign or mark as signature, for example, an asterisk (*), especially when dealing with the preliminary leaves.

To confuse matters further, the term signature is often used to refer not only to the individual signature marks on the printed sheet, but also by extension to the entire sheet, once it has been folded and sewn into the book. In this sense **signature** is a synonym for 'gathering'.

Having established the format of the book through the signature letters, we can then **collate** the book by means of the signatures, ie., examine the leaves of the book to determine that everything is there that should be there. In the case of very early books in particular, reliance cannot be put upon the page numbers as a guide to completeness since the printer often made mistakes in the numbering. Checking the leaves is a much surer guide. If the bibliographer has determined that the book is a quarto he can then count the number of leaves between each separate signature letter. Should he find any number other than four between any pair of letters then he knows he is faced with a peculiarity of some sort. If the number is less than four then it may be that a leaf or two is missing. The only common exceptions to this rule concern the gatherings at the beginning and end of the book. I have already referred to the preliminary leaves, at the front of the book. The final gathering may also consist of an odd number of leaves - six leaves only, for example, in the case of an octavo book. The likely explanation is that there was only enough printed matter to fill twelve pages (six leaves), so the remaining, blank leaves were removed at the time of binding.

Matters of format and signature are most relevant to older books, broadly those printed prior to the early nineteenth century. If your interest is primarily in books of the nineteenth century and later, you may be relieved to know that you need not pay too much attention to them, although they certainly cannot be ignored completely. Variations, complications and oddities in format and signature are far more common in books dating from before about 1800 because they reflect the eccentricities and whims of individual printers. Before this time, printing was still largely a craft process, in other words, a process which allowed large scope for individual expression, and error. With increasing mechanisation of printing from the early nineteenth century onwards, the scope for variation became a great deal more restricted. The importance of the signature, in particular, diminished throughout the nineteenth century as the folding of the sheet was automated - the whole point of the signature in its inception was as an aid to the human hand and eye. Today it survives for the most part only in a vestigial form.

THE PRELIMINARY LEAVES

The **preliminary leaves**, or **prelims** for short, are all those leaves which appear before the text proper, ie., page one of the book. What follows is a description of everything that *might* appear among the preliminary leaves of a book, though to avoid confusion we have, perhaps confusingly, to begin with something which is not a preliminary leaf.

When you open the cover of a book the first thing that normally confronts you is a blank leaf. If the book has been bound in leather or cloth, this first leaf will probably be the **endpaper**. The endpapers are the sheets inserted by the binder at each end of the book, one half of the sheet being pasted to the inside of the cover, the other being free. With the great majority of books the endpaper does not constitute one of the preliminary leaves, since it is put there by the binder and is not the responsibility of the printer. There are a few exceptions to this rule, books in which a spare blank leaf at the beginning of the first gathering and/or the end of the last gathering have been utilised as endpapers for the front and rear covers respectively. (See below for 'blank leaves'). One motive for this procedure was economy.

Endpapers are often of a different paper from the paper on which the book has been printed; sometimes the difference is only slight, but can be detected by feel or by an examination of watermarks. Often the difference is striking, especially with nineteenth-century books, in which the endpapers are frequently made of tinted or marbled paper. Lastly, the collector should be aware that endpapers have often been removed - torn out - at some stage in the life of the book, perhaps because someone was in need of notepaper, perhaps because an inscription was found offensive or disagreeable.

After the endpaper there may be a **blank leaf**, or **blank** for short. The presence of a blank is often the result of the printer not having quite enough material to fill both sides of a sheet when he comes to make up the preliminary leaves. If we take an octavo book as an example (recalling octavo imposition) the matter to be printed might fill fourteen pages only (out of sixteen). Rather than juggle the material around, it would be simpler from the printer's point of view to leave the equivalent of pages one and two empty and start on 'page' 3. In earlier books the blank leaf was often planned, as a protection for the title-leaf against dirt and damage. When the book went for binding the binder might remove the blank or not according to his own whim or the owner's wishes. (One important motive for the binder to remove the blank was the money to be made from selling paper-waste back to paper-makers.) Collectors naturally prefer the blank to be present.

(Blank leaves are often found at the back of the book as well, though such blanks would obviously not form part of the prelims. Very occasionally they are found in the middle of the book, perhaps marking the end of a division in the printed matter. There are also such things as binder's blanks, ie., blank leaves inserted by the binder, in addition to the endpaper, perhaps to bulk out the binding. One way of distinguishing between a printer's blank and a binder's blank is to examine the paper. Quite often, especially with books of the eighteenth century and earlier, the two will display markedly different characteristics - the chain lines might run in different directions; one paper may be laid while the other may be wove - which prove that they must have come from different sheets. Another way of distinguishing a binder's blank from a printer's blank is to check the signing of the first gathering.)

After any blank leaves there might appear a **half-title**. This usually only carries the title of the book, sometimes in abbreviated form if the title is a long one. On one hypothesis, the half-title originated in the sixteenth century as a label for the spine of the book. The half-title, or short title, would be printed on the first leaf. The binder would cut out this half-title and paste it to the spine. With longer titles in particular, the printer would sometimes set the half-title to print down the leaf rather than across it. Books with this peculiar 'half-title' unused and still in place in the book are very occasionally met with. As techniques for lettering the spine developed the practice died out, but by then the half-title had become a traditional part of the preliminary leaves and printers were loath to abandon it.

According to another hypothesis the half-title represents a refinement of the blank to which I have already referred. A leaf was required at the beginning of the book to protect the title-leaf, particularly when the sheets had been folded ready for binding and were left stacked on a shelf; rather than leave it blank, better to print on it some indication of what the book was so that the sheets could be identified, before binding, without being picked up and handled. The half-title in this form was often discarded by the binder when he came to bind the book, much to the annoyance of present-day collectors. In the course of the nineteenth century the half-title was often used to carry further information, usually on the verso - perhaps details of other publications by the author or from the same publisher. It thus became more of an integral part of the book.

After the half-title there may appear a **frontispiece**, or frontis for short. The frontispiece is an illustration of some sort - perhaps a portrait of the author, an illustration of a scene in the book, a map or a plan. Very often the frontispiece is engraved, and as such constitutes a separate entity from the printed sheet since printed by an entirely different process, one which will be dealt with in the chapter on illustration.

The frontispiece generally appears immediately before, and facing the title-page. The title-page is obviously the most important of the preliminary leaves, indeed it is the only essential part. It gives the book's full title; it usually gives the name of the author and any editors, translators, etc who might have been involved in the production. It should give details of the edition, the place and date of publication, the publisher and perhaps the printer. More detailed discussion of the title-page is reserved for a separate chapter.

A relatively uncommon feature of the prelims is a second title leaf. This leaf is purely decorative. It is often engraved, like the frontis, and appears immediately before, and sometimes facing, the title leaf (and therefore between the title leaf and any frontis). It will carry the title of the book, sometimes the author and publisher, often in a decorative script. Since its purpose is decorative it will almost always carry an illustration of some sort. This second title is sometimes referred to as an 'extra' or 'additional' title, to distinguish it from the main title. If it is engraved it might be described as an 'extra - or additional - engraved title'. The main title might then be described as the 'printed title'. In the nineteenth century publishers would sometimes describe this second title as a 'vignette title', which is not to be confused with a title vignette. A **vignette** is a small illustration which occupies only a part of the page. It is usually engraved, as opposed to printed.

After the title-page there may appear a **dedication**. This could take the form of a letter, a piece of verse or even quite a long essay, in which the author dedicates the book to someone, usually someone rich and powerful, often someone who has helped in the production of the book, if only by offering patronage or protection.

The dedication can sometimes be helpful in elucidating the circumstances surrounding the book's publication, or peculiarities about the book. An example is Aylmer Bourne Lambert's *A description of the genus Pinus ...*, first issued in 1803 with 43 botanical illustrations of parts of plants and trees, and a dedication to the botanist Sir Joseph Banks. By the time a second edition was contemplated, in 1832, Banks was dead. This new edition contained an additional set of illustrations of complete trees, and a dedication to William IV, a monarch with an active interest in forest trees. It is difficult not to construe the additional illustrations as a tribute to the new dedicatee.

A much more blatantly opportunist use of the dedication is recorded by Desmond Flower in his collection of Voltaire's works. One copy only of Voltaire's play *Oedipe* (1719) is recorded with the original dedication removed and replaced by a printed dedication to King George I. This copy must have been presented to the king himself, who presented Voltaire in return with a gold watch. It is perhaps too fanciful to read into this incident a presentiment on the part of Voltaire that a few years later he would be forced into exile in England to avoid imprisonment in the Bastille.

There may be an **advertisement** among the prelims, possibly an advertisement in our sense of the word but much more likely 'advertisement' in an archaic sense of 'notice', in which the author or publisher draws the reader's attention to some peculiarity of the book, the circumstances of its writing or publication, or some change from a previous edition.

We are familiar today with the Foreword, the Preface, the Contents and the List of Illustrations. What we are not familiar with is the **subscribers' list**. In the eighteenth century in particular it was not unusual for an author to assume responsibility for the publication of his own work. The most common method of financing this method of publication was by subscription. The author would solicit orders for the book prior to publication in order to defray all or part of the expenses of producing it. The names of those who 'subscribed' would be printed in the subscribers' list. As with the dedication, the subscribers' list can sometimes yield useful information about the circumstances of the book's production.

A leaf which gives **directions to the binder** sometimes appears among the preliminary leaves, though it may appear at the end of the book. As the term implies, these 'directions' inform the binder how the book is to be bound, usually with reference to the positioning of engraved illustrations and the like. As often as not these instructions were blithely ignored, with the binder placing the illustrations wherever he fancied, much to the chagrin of the reader and, subsequently, the collector.

The term **fly-leaf** needs to be treated with some caution. I have noticed it used at one time or another to refer to four different items: (1) the front free endpaper (ie., that part of the endpaper not pasted down), (2) a blank leaf inserted by the binder, (3) a blank leaf that is part of a gathering, (4) the half-title. Since alternative terms are available it is probably best avoided.

A relatively unusual item of the prelims is the **divisional title**, a kind of secondary half-title which will occasionally be found after all the other prelims and immediately before the text proper. Divisional titles also occur, perhaps more naturally, in the body of the text, to mark divisions.

Finally, there is the **errata leaf**, a list of printer's errors. While an errata leaf may appear among the prelims, it is equally often found at the end of the book. Then there may not be a separate leaf for the errata; the list might be printed on the otherwise blank verso of another leaf. Sometimes the errata may be printed on a small piece of paper - an **errata slip** - stuck in between two leaves.

THE TITLE-PAGE

Booksellers almost universally abbreviate 'title-page' or 'title-leaf' to 'title', as in the expressions 'lacks title', or 'title stained'. A secondary use, not confined to the trade, is the use of 'title' to mean a book, as in 'another popular title by Charlotte M. Yonge'. Strictly, the title-*page* refers to the actual printed matter, while the title-*leaf* describes the physical piece of paper.

Before the invention of printing it was the practice in manuscript production for the scribe to begin the first page of the text with the title of the work and a statement as to authorship. This statement in known as the **incipit** (from the Latin verb for begin) and in English texts was written 'Heir begynneth'. The text of the work would follow immediately on this statement; thus there was no separate title-leaf. It was also the practice of the scribes to finish off their manuscripts by giving the date and place of production at the *end* of the work. From this practice is derived the word **colophon**, which is Greek for 'finishing stroke'. The first printers not unnaturally took over both these practices, so the information we would expect to find on the title-page is split between the first and last pages of the text.

The colophon is of particular interest to bibliographers. It would consist of the printer's name with the date and place of printing. (This information is collectively known as the **imprint**.) Sometimes these details would be accompanied by the printer's **device**, a design or ornament which the printer adopted as his logo or trademark.

Occasionally, particularly with very early books, the colophon would be expanded to include a short statement from the printer-publisher begging the reader's indulgence for any short-comings in the work, the kind of statement we would expect to find nowadays in the prefatory material. Here

Christopher Plantin's device

John Day's device

is part of Caxton's colophon to his edition of Ralph Higden's *Polychronicon* (1482), a world history:

'And here I make an ende of this lytel werke as nygh as I can fynde [...] prayenge all them that shall see this symple werke to pardone me of my symple and rude wrytynge. Ended the second day of Juyll the xxii yere of the regne of kynge Edward the fourth and of the Incarnacion of our Lord a thousand four honderd foure score and tweyne, Fynnysshed per Caxton'.

'Colophon' is occasionally mistakenly used today to refer to the printer's or publisher's device on the title-page.

It wasn't long before the need for a title-page as we understand it came to be recognised and by the early sixteenth century it was well established. However, the use of the colophon persisted well into the same century. It is not uncommon to find a book with both a title-page and a colophon, and it is not uncommon to find the information they give does not agree. (The most common area of disagreement is over the place and date of printing, which is generally the date of publication as well. A second bookseller may have acquired some unsold copies of the book at a later date and issued them with a new title-page bearing his own details and a new date. However, it would be considered too expensive and troublesome to reprint the last leaf of the text bearing the colophon.

The title-page has undergone many transformations. In the very earliest examples, it consisted simply of the name of the book or a list of its contents, sometimes with the name of the author. During the early sixteenth century it began to take over the function of the colophon, with the addition of the printer's name and the date of printing. In the later sixteenth century we see the evolution of the decorated title-page, with a wood-cut border or more elaborate ornament. The decorated title-page achieved its highest expression in the seventeenth century, when the entire title-page might be engraved, with the details of title and author almost lost in the elaborate design. This is known as an **engraved title** In later centuries, the eighteenth and nineteenth in particular, decoration frequently took the form of a title vignette. (It is important to distinguish between a vignette and a device, the former being purely decorative, the latter serving as an identifying trade-mark. Vignettes, or vignette illustrations, sometimes appear in the body of the book, at the beginning and end of chapters. In this position they are often known, respectively, as a **head-piece** and a **tail-piece**.)

THE MASSE DIS-PLAYED.

VVRITTEN IN FRENCH
by Mr JOHN BEDE, advocate to
the Parliament of Paris, *and
now tranſlated into
Engliſh.*

Tertull. de Oration. Cap. 12.
Huiuſmodi non religioni, ſed ſuperſtitioni deputantur, affectata & coacta, & curioſi potius quam rationalis officij, certè vel eo coercenda quod Gentilibus adæquent.

AC: OX

AT OXFORD,
Printed by JOHN LICHFIELD, and JAMES SHORT, Printers to the famous Vniverſitie. 1619.

An early seventeenth-century title-page from a work printed at Oxford. The first permanent printing press was established in Oxford in 1584.

In the later seventeenth century and in the eighteenth century decoration of the title-page was often confined to printing the title in red and black. (In manuscripts and early printed books the initital letter of each heading was often either written or printed in red. This practice is known as **rubrication**.)

From the sixteenth to the eighteenth centuries it was common practice to give not simply the title of the book but what amounted to a resumé of the contents - the kind of information we would nowadays expect to find on the dust-jacket. This development sprang in part from the fact that the title-page was considered an advertisement for the book; copies of the title-leaf were often printed and distributed independently of the book itself. A development of the title-page as advertisement occurred during the nineteenth century, when the publisher would detail some of the author's other works, often without actually naming the author him or herself. (Charlotte M. Yonge, already mentioned, would frequently be identified on the title-page of her works simply as 'Author of The Heir of Redclyffe', a reference to her most popular work - or 'title'.)

The idea of the publisher as we understand it did not develop until the second quarter of the nineteenth century. Up till then, the function of the publisher was often undertaken by the bookseller, who would commission the book and oversee its printing. (In very early times, the role of bookseller and printer were also combined.) Thus the title-page would contain details of those from whom the book could be obtained. A number of booksellers might combine to publish a book, and then the title-page would list all their names and addresses.

Curiously, the only information that might be said *always* to appear on the title-page is the title itself. While the author's name generally appears, it doesn't always. Sometimes the author was considered well-known already and didn't need to be identified; sometimes the author desired anonymity, for a variety of reasons. During the religious and social upheavals of the sixteenth century it was often safer for an author to remain anonymous, while in the eighteenth century the writing of books was considered too close to 'trade', and trade was not the occupation of a gentleman.

As well as being anonymous, books were often published pseudonymously (George Eliot, Lewis Carroll, Mark Twain, Currer Bell). In bibliographies and reference works in general such authors may be listed under their pseudonyms or under their real names (Mary Ann Evans, Charles L. Dodgson, Samuel L. Clemens, Charlotte Bronte). Sometimes the fact that a name is pseudonymous may be obvious (Tom Tittletattle), sometimes less so. The most comprehensive reference work on anonymous and pseudonymous works is Samuel Halkett and John Laing's *Dictionary of Anonymous and Pseudonymous Literature*, first published in the 1880's and since revised and supplemented.

The date of publication is information that one would expect to find on the title-page but often it does not appear there. Occasionally the date appears elsewhere in the book, in modern books, for example, on the verso of the title. Quite often the book is not dated at all. (A cataloguer may well indicate this fact by using the abbreviation **n.d.** - 'no date'. The similar abbreviation for 'no place' [of printing] is **n.p.**) With reprints, particularly facsimile reprints, the original title-page is often reprinted in its entirety, without comment and without any indication that it is a reprint, no later imprint giving details of who was responsible for the facsimile.

With Continental productions, particularly French books, the imprint, including the date of publication, is often to be found at the *end* of the book.

If the book is undated a little detective work is necessary. A preface in the book might well be dated, and while this is by no means an absolutely sure guide to dating, it can provide a good indication. The presence of advertisements can sometimes provide a guide. In the nineteenth century in particular publishers frequently bound in catalogues of their stock at the end of each book, and these catalogues would usually be dated. The only sure way to date an undated book is to check it against a bibliography, either a specialist bibliography of the subject or author, or against the catalogue of the British Library. If a bookseller has discovered through research the date of an undated book he will generally provide that information in a catalogue description, but in square brackets -[ ].

Finally, even when a date is given it may not be correct! Tobias Smollett was an eighteenth-century writer, one of whose works, *The Expedition of Humphrey Clinker*, was, according to the title-page, first issued in 1671, some fifty years before Smollett's birth. The date should have read '1771'. Even a number of later editions were mis-dated, with 1673 for 1773 and 1685 for 1785.

A typical egraved title-page of the seventeenth century from Sir Walter Raleigh's "History of the World".

A PRACTICAL

GRAMMAR

OF THE

Engliſh TONGUE:

Or, a Rational and Eaſy

INTRODUCTION

To Speaking and Writing *ENGLISH*
Correctly and Properly;

Peculiarly adapted to the NATURE and Genius of the LANGUAGE; and free from the hard and unneceſſary Terms of the LATIN *Rudiments.*

The Whole treated of in expreſſive Terms and familiar Style, and in the moſt natural and inſtructive Method, *viz.* That of QUESTION and ANSWER.

Deſign'd for the Uſe of SCHOOLS.

This Work tho' calculated chiefly for the Uſe of the FAIR SEX, and ſuch as require only an ENGLISH Education, may yet be a uſeful Foundation to thoſe who are deſign'd for higher Studies.

By *WILLIAM LOUGHTON,*
School-Maſter at *Kenſington.*

The SEVENTH EDITION, with CORRECTIONS and IMPROVEMENTS.

To which is annex'd,

An INTRODUCTION to the ART of WRITING, illuſtrated with ſeveral *Specimens* of all the uſual Hands, curiouſly *engraved* by Mr. BICKHAM.

LONDON:
Printed for B. DOD at the *Bible* and *Key* in *Ave-Mary-Lane* near Stationers-Hall. M. DCC. XLIX.
(Price 1 *s.* 6 *d.* or 15 *s.* a Dozen, for the Uſe of Schools.)

A typical eighteenth-century title-page, showing the use of the title-page to provide the blurb which nowadays would be found perhaps on the dust-jacket. Note the name of the bookseller/publisher and the address of his place of business.

C A T U L L I,

T I B U L L I,

E T

P R O P E R T I I

O P E R A

B I R M I N G H A M I AE:

Typis J O H A N N I S B A S K E R V I L L E.

M D C C L X X I I.

The title-page from one of John Baskerville's productions (1772) exemplifying his austerely elegant lay-out, far different from the cramped title-page of the "Grammar" by Loughton (opposite) and prefiguring the style of much twentieth-century typography, for example, that of the work by James Joyce (overleaf), printed in 1932.

TWO TALES OF SHEM AND SHAUN

FRAGMENTS FROM
WORK IN PROGRESS

BY

JAMES JOYCE

LONDON
FABER AND FABER
24 RUSSELL SQUARE

The place of publication can also give rise to problems. Just as an author might decide upon anonymity as the better part of valour, so the printer-publisher might decide, in the case of a particularly contentious work, that it would be judicious to attempt to throw the authorities of the track by giving a false place of printing. Some of Voltaire's works, for example, were printed in Amsterdam according to the title-page but in fact printed in Paris.

Books of erotica were frequently given outlandish, obviously fictitious places of printing. 'Cosmopolis' is a firm favourite among publishers of such work.

A difficulty with books written in Latin, especially earlier books, concerns the Latinisation of the place name. Every place of printing had a Latin version of its name and these can sometimes prove difficult to translate. A few of the more common are as follows:

Argentina or Argentoratum: Strassburg

Augusta Trinobantum: London

Aurelia Allobrogum: Geneva

Basilae: Basle

Colonia: Cologne

Eboracum: York

Lugdunum Batavorum: Leyden

Luetia: Paris

Mediolanum: Milan

Venetiae: Venice

'Constantinople' is almost always a fictitious imprint.

Roman numerals can also be a problem for the tyro. We have already met them in connection with the numbering of the preliminary leaves and of signatures, but they are also commonly used for the date of the book. The principle of roman numbering is simple to grasp, even though the number itself can look quite intimidating. Overleaf there is a list of some sample numbers and dates.

i	1
ii	2
iii	3
iv	4 (1 before 5)
v	5
vi	6 (5 and 1)
vii	7
viii	8
ix	9 (1 before 10)
x	10
xi	11
xii	12
xx	20 (10 and 10)
xxi	21
xxx	30
xl	40 (10 before 50)
xli	41
l	50
lx	60
lxx	70
lxxx	80
xc	90 (10 before 100)
c	100
cc	200
ccc	300
cd	400 (100 before 500)
d	500
m	1000

MDCXXIV	1624
MDLXXXVIII	1588
MCMLX	1960
MDCCXC	1790
MCDLXXV	1475
MDCCCII	1802
MDCXCII	1692
MDCCXLIII	1743
MDCCCLVII	1857
MCMXCV	1995

Collation and Description

'Collation' has two rather different, though related meanings. In one sense, if a book has been 'collated with another copy', it means that book has been compared with another, presumably perfect copy, leaf for leaf. The check will reveal whether or not the first copy is complete. In the second sense of the word, 'collation' means the bibliographical description of the book. To give the collation of the book is to describe it in a conventional formula using standard terminology. It is this second sense of the word that concerns us here. Some knowledge of the principles involved is essential if booksellers' catalogues and bibliographies are to be understood.

Books may be collated by their gatherings, which entails detailing their signatures; they may be collated by their pages, or by their leaves. Collation by pages is the most common, collation by leaves comparatively rare. Collation by signature tends to be reserved for earlier books, as the most reliable form of collation. The more expensive early books, in particular, tend to be collated by signature. However, this is not a hard and fast rule. Individual booksellers and bibliographers have different preferences; some booksellers specialising in the most expensive antiquarian books now prefer to collate by leaves.

Collation by Gathering

Collation by gathering is simply a systematic description of the signatures, or gatherings, of the book. As we saw in the previous chapter, the practice of most printers was and is to print the text proper of the work first, and the preliminary leaves afterwards. As a result of this practice, when the printer signed the gatherings he would often reserve the letter A for the preliminary leaves and begin the signing of the text with the letter B. Again, as we saw when looking at signatures, the signing of the preliminary leaves is often peculiar, not least because they may comprise an odd number of leaves. The title-page itself is almost never signed. Sometimes no signature letter appears anywhere on the preliminary leaves. For the sake of simplicity, the following examples may be taken to disregard unsigned preliminary leaves. (Remember that the alphabet for signatures contains only 23 letters.)

1) Folio, B-Aa
A folio book, with 23 gatherings of 2 leaves each, giving 46 leaves or 92 pages

2) Folio, a-n6
A folio book in sixes, with 13 gatherings of 6 leaves each, giving 78 leaves or 156 pages

3) 4to, A-D4
A quarto book, with 4 gatherings of 4 leaves each, giving 16 leaves or 32 pages.

4) 4to, A-P8, Q4
A quarto book in eights, with 15 gatherings of 8 leaves each and 1 gathering of 4 leaves, giving 124 leaves or 248 pages

5) 8vo, A-T8
An octavo book, with 19 gatherings of 8 leaves each, giving 152 leaves or 304 pages

6) 8vo, B-Gg8
An octavo book, with 29 gatherings of 8 leaves each, giving 232 leaves or 464 pages.

7) 8vo, A-R8 S4
An octavo book, with 17 gatherings of 8 leaves each and 1 gathering of 4 leaves, giving 140 leaves or 280 pages.

8) 12mo, a12 A-L12
A 12mo book, with 12 gatherings of 12 leaves each, giving 144 leaves or 288 pages.

In all the examples above we can assume that all the gatherings are perfectly regular, with nothing untoward in any of them. (Examples 4 and 7 have a smaller than standard gathering at the end only.) The description '8vo,

A-T8', without qualification, can be taken to mean that each gathering consists of 8 leaves. If there is a peculiarity to a gathering in the middle of the book the cataloguer will - or should - make the fact plain. The description '8vo, A-F8 G4 H-T8' tells us that, though an octavo book, the gathering G has only 4 leaves instead of the expected 8. Having indicated as much, the cataloguer may well go on to explain why this is, and whether it implies any defect in the book. (It need not imply any defect. For example, the book may consist of two parts printed independently.)

Occasionally, especially with the preliminary leaves, one or two leaves may be unsigned and it may be impossible to infer to which gathering they belong. A conventional sign to indicate such unsigned leaves is the Greek letter Π (pi).

Having given the collation, the cataloguer may then use the signatures to indicate any defects or peculiarities of particular leaves. 'F4 shaved' means that the fourth leaf of gathering F has been shaved, ie., cut too close to the text by the binder. 'Kk6 blank' means just what it says - that leaf contains no printed matter.

Collation by Page

Collation by pages is much commoner than collation by signatures, and somewhat easier to understand. In this type of collation, the cataloguer simply gives the number of pages in the book, or the book's **pagination**. In English printing it is common practice among printers to use roman numerals for the preliminary leaves and anything else that is extraneous to the main body of text, and arabic numerals for the text itself. This distinction is brought out in the collation (**pp** is the usual abbreviation for 'pages').

1) 8vo, pp vi+398
An octavo book, with 6 preliminary pages and 398 pages of text.

2) 8vo, pp xviii+206+viii
An octavo book, with 18 preliminary pages, 206 pages of text and 8 pages at the end, perhaps an index or appendix.

Very often, not all the preliminary pages will be numbered. If the cataloguer wants to draw attention to this he will do so by the use of square brackets - [ ]. (Square brackets are in general use to indicate some detail or piece of information which the cataloguer or bibliographer is providing for the reader of the entry, but which is not actually printed on the page.)

3) 8vo, [iv]+450
An octavo book with 4 unnumbered preliminary pages and 450 pages of text.

Where some of the preliminary pages are numbered and some are not, many cataloguers will simply count up the total number and give that number without the use of square brackets. The fact that some are numbered and some are not is so common and so well known that attention seldom needs to be drawn to it.

However, a punctilious description of numbered and unnumbered pages might runs as follows:

4) 8vo, pp [i-iv]+v-xv+[xvi]+[1]-272.

When the last leaf of the prelims is not numbered - regardless of whether some or all of the earlier leaves were numbered or not - some cataloguers will give the total number of prelims in square brackets. Thus example (3) above might bear a different interpretation: a book with, perhaps, pages two and three of the prelims numbered, but the final, fourth page unnumbered.

Occasionally, while retaining the distinction between roman and arabic numerals, the printer will employ a single continuous numerical sequence, instead of beginning the first page of the text with the number 1:

5) 8vo, pp vii+8-272.

Collation by Leaf

Collation by leaves is much the least common of the three methods of collation. It was quite a common practice in early printing for the printer to number individual *leaves* rather than pages. A specialised sense of the word **folio** is that of a leaf thus numbered, ie., on the recto only. From this is derived the term for this type of collation, **foliation**. The abbreviation for 'folios' in this sense is **ff**.

1) 4to, ff 64
A quarto book of 64 leaves - or folios - giving 128 pages.

A practice of a few cataloguers involves combining elements of collation by leaf and collation by pages. If the book is paginated the cataloguer will give the number of pages in the usual way but then indicate unnumbered preliminary leaves by leaf or folio.

2) ff[2], pp 379
A book with two preliminary leaves (four pages) and 379 pages of text.

Description

The collation of the book will be followed by its description. My example is a book by Leonardo Lessius, *Sir Walter Raleigh's Ghost; or, His Apparition to an intimate Friend, willing him to translate into English this Learned Book of L. Lessius,* published in 1651.

The book's format is 12mo, and it collates:

12mo. [A12] B-R11.

In the first gathering - A - only A4 and A5 are signed, but the attempt to indicate this would make the notation unnecessarily complicated. Note that the last gathering consists of eleven leaves only.

The description runs as follows (recall that 'r' and 'v' are the abbreviations, respectively, of 'recto' and 'verso'):

A1r title; A1v blank; A2r-A2v publisher's Dedication; A3r- A3v publisher's advertisements; A4r-A5v 'The Apparition' (ie., a sort of Foreword); A6r-A7v 'The Translator to the Reader'; A8r- A9r 'The Table of Chapters'; A9v-A12v 'The Author's Preface'; B- R11 text.

Compare this with a collation and description of the same book by pages, rather than signatures:

12mo. Pp [xxiv] + 382.

[i] title; [ii] blank; [iii-iv] Dedication; [v-vi] advertisements; [vii-x] 'The Apparition'; [xi-xiv] 'The Translator to the Reader'; [xv-xvii] 'The Table of Chapters'; [xviii-xxiv] 'The Author's Preface'; 1-382 text.

These are the types of exhaustive description to be expected in catalogues of relatively early printed books, particularly the rarer and more expensive items, though practice does vary from one bookseller to another. It is also, as importantly, the form of description frequently met with in bibliographies. The aim of a bibliography, especially an author bibliography, is to provide a definitive bibliographical description of the individual works of a particular author, among other things so that copies of the author's books can be checked against the description to determine their status - is everything there that should be there? is it a first edition? a reprint? a later issue?

In some cases it may be necessary or desirable not merely to note the content of the title-page but also to give a picture of how the content is laid out. Obviously, the best method is by reproducing the title-page in facsimile, but very often this is not possible and then bibliographers must rely on a standard descriptive formula, in which the whole contents are listed, with line breaks symbolised by vertical or angled lines and square brackets enclosing the bibliographer's description of any decorative or explanatory matter. The degree to which the different sizes and varieties of type can be reproduced is obviously dependent upon the facilities available to the printer.

Opposite is such a description of the title-page of a little work for children by Charlotte Smith. The actual title-page is reproduced for purposes of comparison.

T & A Hill.

Rambles Farther:

A

CONTINUATION

OF

RURAL WALKS:

IN DIALOGUES.

INTENDED

FOR THE USE OF YOUNG PERSONS.

By CHARLOTTE SMITH.

IN TWO VOLUMES.

VOL. I.

LONDON:

Printed for T. CADELL Jun. and W. DAVIES,
(Succeſſors to Mr. CADELL,) in the STRAND.

1796.

Rambles Farther: /A/CONTINUATION/OF/RURAL WALKS:/ IN DIALOGUES./INTENDED/FOR THE USE OF YOUNG PERSONS./ [lozenge rule]/By CHARLOTTE SMITH./[lozenge rule]/IN TWO VOLUMES./VOL. I./[thick rule over thin rule]/ LONDON:/ Printed for T. CADELL Jun. and W. DAVIES,/ (Successors to Mr. CADELL,) in the STRAND./1796.

EDITION, IMPRESSION, STATE AND ISSUE

There is a degree of looseness in the application of these terms among booksellers, bibliographers and publishers themselves. What follows is an attempt at a strict definition of each.

An **edition** comprises all those copies of a book printed from one setting of type. As long as the type is left *standing* (ie., as arranged by the compositor in the chase) any number of copies may be printed off, over any period of time - they will all form part of the same edition.

An **impression** consists of all those copies of a book printed from one setting of type in any one operation (the actual printing process may take several hours or several days). Thus within an edition there might be any number of impressions. There is no theoretical limit to the number of impressions which any given edition may contain.

Modern practice is to note the sequence of impressions on the verso of the title-page ('First edition, second impression'). By convention, 'first edition' has come to mean 'first edition, first impression', so the expression 'first impression' is seldom used. An interesting point about modern publishing is the practice of printing several different impressions before the book is actually published. In the run up to publication the publisher becomes persuaded that he can sell more copies than he originally ordered from the printer and so decides to have more copies printed. These printings constitute different impressions and are noted in the book as 'second impression before publication'.

The problem of distinguishing editions from impressions only really arises from the late eighteenth century onwards. Up till then the cost of type made it uneconomic for the printer to leave type standing in the hope that more copies of the book would be called for. As soon as the print run was finished the type would be *distributed* (ie., broken up) and used elsewhere. If more copies of the book were required a new set of type would be put together. But this printing would constitute a new edition, since made from a new setting of type.

Towards the end of the eighteenth century printers began to adopt the practice of leaving the type standing for a few weeks, in case more copies of the book were required. But publishers were often in the habit of describing subsequent printings from the one setting of type as different *editions*!

For some people the idea of the 'same setting of type' is extended conceptually to include facsimiles.

The earliest facsimile is the **stereotype**. The stereotype was used sporadically throughout the eighteenth century, more generally in the nineteenth. A stereotype plate was prepared by making a mould of the block of type as set up by the compositor in plaster, papier-mâché or similar material. A solid block of type-metal was then cast from this mould, and used for printing. The advantage of the stereotype method, in the eighteenth century in particular, was that the original blocks of type could be distributed as soon as the stereotype plate had been made and the type used again for another book. A disadvantage was that corrections to the stereotype plate could only be made with some difficulty.

A second form of facsimile is the photo-lithographic form of reproduction, where the reprinting does not actually involve type at all. A common application of this method currently popular is the printing of facsimile editions of sixteenth and seventeenth century books.

An **issue** may be defined as all those copies of a book put onto the market at any one time. Separate batches of the book marketed at discrete intervals would constitute separate issues. (An issue may or may not be co-extensive with an impression or an edition.) In practice, more particularly with modern books, there is nothing to distinguish books of one issue from books of any other. The question of issue becomes important for the bookseller and collector when some alteration has been made to the book between one issue and another. Here we become concerned with the **issue point**, ie., what distinguishes any given issue from other issues.

Three Men in a Boat

(TO SAY NOTHING OF THE DOG)

BY

JEROME K. JEROME

AUTHOR OF

"IDLE THOUGHTS OF AN IDLE FELLOW,"

"STAGE LAND," ETC.

Illustrations by A. Frederics.

BRISTOL

J. W. ARROWSMITH, 11 QUAY STREET

LONDON

SIMPKIN, MARSHALL, HAMILTON, KENT & Co. LIMITED

1889

All rights reserved

An issue point. The title-page of a later issue of Jerome K. Jerome's "Three Men in a Boat". The first edition, first issue does not have the numeral in the Bristol address ('J.W. Arrowsmith, Quay Street').

A typical example of an issue point might involve a **cancel** (one leaf of the original text proves to be defective or offensive in some way, perhaps containing a serious misprint or a libel, and has to be removed and replaced with a newly printed leaf). Copies of the book with the cancel leaf would then be described as 'second issue'. Or it may be that after a book has gone on sale it becomes necessary to add to copies yet unsold some explanatory material in the form of an appendix. Copies with this new material would constitute a separate issue. Again, it isn't unusual for different copies of the same edition to have publisher's catalogues bearing different dates bound in at the end. The only inference to be drawn is that copies with the later-dated catalogue were issued later and therefore constitute a 'later issue'. An extreme example of this is Ludwig Wittgenstein's *Tractatus Logico-Philosophicus*. The English edition was first issued in 1922 and did not meet with overwhelming success. Copies of the same sheets - not a new impression, but the 'first edition, first impression' - were still being bound up and issued some fifteen years later but with an up-to-date catalogue.

Perhaps the publisher decides, after a lapse of time, to reissue some of the original sheets with a different title-leaf bearing a new date. This is, strictly, a new *issue* of the book, though the publisher would often describe it as a new *edition*. One motive for this would be to imply to the book-buying public that the book had been more of a success than was in fact the case!

Probably the most famous example of an issue point involves *Alice in Wonderland*. Lewis Carroll objected to the first set of illustrations for the book produced by John Tenniell and wanted them redrawn. His publisher, however, had already begun printing the book with the offending illustrations. The copies already printed were rounded up and the book reprinted with the new illustrations. However, a few copies with the original illustrations had already got into circulation, and these constitute the first edition, first issue. Copies of the book with the second set of illustrations constitute the first edition, second issue. Copies of the first issue are extremely rare and needless to say fetch far more money than copies of the second issue. An additional piquancy is the fact that the publisher had already shipped to the U.S.A. sheets with the offending illustrations, and these he was unwilling to recall. So the first U.S. edition of the book bears the original illustrations, but since printed in large numbers is not particularly rare.

If a bookseller describes a book as being the 'first issue' then it is presumed that there exists objective evidence to determine priority between the various issues of the work. If no such evidence exists the bookseller might employ the expression 'variant issue', though this would still imply a knowledge of the standard from which the particular copy under discussion varies in some way. An even less committed stance would see the bookseller merely detailing the issue point while making no statement about the question of priority.

The matter of issue may arise in connection with the dust-jacket of the book rather than the book itself. The same book may have different dust-jackets, designed by the same or different artists, to coincide with different issues of the book. Thus a cataloguer might refer to a 'first issue dust-jacket' or a 'remainder dust-jacket'. The jacket on Evelyn Waugh's novel *Scoop* (1938), a book about the mores of journalists and newspaper proprietors, had to be altered after publication upon the threat of legal proceedings by a national newspaper whose proprietor thought the design resembled too closely the masthead of his own paper. Thus there are two issues of the jacket.

Different **states** of the same edition result from more minor alterations to the book *while it is printing*. Copies of the book with and without the alteration will then be put on sale simultaneously. Different states of the same book might typically arise as a result of a minor typographical mistake being corrected part-way through the printing. An example is to be found in Joseph Conrad's *The Arrow of Gold* (1919). In some copies the letter A in the **running title** (the title of the work to be found across the top of every page) on page 67 has dropped slightly as a result of the type-letter being knocked out of place. At some point in the printing this fault was noticed, the machines stopped, the type set back in place and the printing resumed. Thus there are two states of the novel to be found, one with the 'dropped letter' and one without.

A more bibliographically bizarre case of different states concerns one of the Christmas books of Charles Dickens. *The Battle of Life* (1846) was issued with an engraved title. Four distinct states of this title have been identified, involving slight alterations in the design, a broken letter and variations in the heaviness of the type. Some half-dozen copies of the book with the first state of the engraved title have been located, and one was recently offered for sale at £30,000. 'Fourth state' copies are the most common and sell for around £100.

A further example of a state might involve a book's illustrations. The engraved plate from which the illustration was printed might have shown signs of wear during the printing; the presses might have been stopped, the engraving retouched and the printing begun again. Such an interference would result in two states of the illustration and, by extension, of the book. In practice, it might require an expert to distinguish one state from another.

I opened this chapter by suggesting that there is a degree of looseness in the application of these terms. 'State' and 'issue', in particular, are often used extremely loosely - one bookseller's issue is another's state. With the example just cited of the Conrad novel, some booksellers might describe copies with the dropped letter A as 'first issue' on the grounds that these copies were, presumably, printed before those copies with the correction. However, this is to ignore the fact that all copies were issued simultaneously.

(As a demonstration of how extreme this sort of bibliographical excursus can become we may imagine the following: that the letter A dropped only after printing had begun. The presses were stopped, the type set back in place and then printing recommenced. Thus there would actually be *three* states of the book: (1) with the letter in the correct position before it dropped; (2) with the letter dropped; (3) with the letter in the correct position after it had been replaced. How one would distinguish the first state from the third I don't know, but that is the sort of challenge beloved of the fanaticist in these matters.)

What is at stake in all this is the question of priority. The collector is interested in determining the question of which came first. Having decided the question he or she is, generally, much more interested in acquiring a copy of the first edition (first impression), first issue or first state rather than the second or the third.

First Edition, Limited Edition and Proof Copy

The reason for linking a discussion of first editions and limited editions is the fact that both terms are generally known outside the trade and both are often misunderstood, at least in their implications. With both there is a general perception that they imply scarcity and therefore confer value, or added value. In most cases, regrettably, this is not so.

The First Edition

The most common misconception about first editions is that the status of 'first edition' bestows value *per se*. ("It *must* be worth something! Look, it's a first edition. It says so!") Unfortunately, this is not so. If it were, every bookseller would be a millionaire several times over. The fact is that the majority of books in circulation are first editions - there was never any demand for a second. If an author is esteemed, a first edition of his or her work may well command a premium over any other edition; if the author is not esteemed, the fact of a given copy being a first edition is neither here nor there as far as value is concerned. There has to be a foundation - of desirability, worth, 'collectability' - before the 'first edition factor' can come into play.

It may be advisable, before reading further, to look again at the chapter dealing with editions and impressions. Some aspects of that discussion will be repeated here, with a slightly different emphasis. The **first edition** for booksellers and collectors may be defined as the first impression of the first edition. The term 'first edition', without qualification, is always taken to mean 'first impression of the first edition'. This is important to bear in mind since for the collector of modern first editions in particular a second impression of the first edition, while in all other respects identical to the first impression, is condemned by the addition of those two innocuous words to perdition. A 'second impression' is almost always worth little or nothing, whatever the value of a first. *Almost* always ... as with every rule there are exceptions, but in this case they are few and far between. Only if the price of the first edition is so horrendously high as to put copies beyond the reach of many collectors will the second or early impressions have some modest value. An example is Tolkien's *Lord of the Rings*. First editions now fetch thousands of pounds; early impressions may be marked at a hundred or two.

The collector of **modern firsts** - fiction, poetry and plays of, roughly, the last sixty to eighty years - represents perhaps the starkest instance of the stress on *priority* (a second impression is by definition a later printing, therefore not the first, therefore not desirable). With modern publishing practice many thousands of copies of the same work may be issued, from the same setting of type, identical to each other in every respect apart from the note as to impression. To the non-collector these distinctions may seem trivial but to the collector they are all.

The principle of priority applies throughout every field of the book collecting. Everything being equal - and of course things may *not* be equal - a first edition is always to be preferred to a later edition.

There are a number of terms in general use which employ the expression 'first edition' with some sort of qualification to indicate the first appearance of a book in a particular form. 'First authorised edition' would imply that there had previously been an *un*authorised edition, even a pirated edition. Eighteenth century writers were particularly prone to attacks of this kind upon their integrity. International laws of copyright have to a large extent eradicated the problem in modern times.

'First edition in book form' is used of works which made their first appearance in some other form, most commonly in periodicals, as was the case with many of the great nineteenth-century novelists, or in **part form**. Many of Charles Dickens' novels were first issued in monthly or fortnightly parts. When publication was complete the work would immediately be reissued in conventional book form. (Needless to say, the value of a copy 'bound from the parts') is substantially higher than the 'first edition in book form'.)

'First separate edition' implies that the material was first published elsewhere as part of a larger work. 'First illustrated edition' is self-explanatory, while 'first English edition' is almost - it might mean the first edition in England, as opposed, for example, to the U.S.A., or it might mean the first edition in English. 'First thus' often suggests a degree of mild desperation on the part of the bookseller, trying to find a selling point for an otherwise unsaleable book. It may be the first appearance of the book with a preface by someone of note or with some other minor alteration or addition. 'True first' might suggest, among other possibilities, that the bookseller is at odds with the bibliographical establishment, who have conferred the title 'first edition' on some other edition.

'First trade edition' implies that there was published simultaneously or a little while before another, special edition not intended for general distribution. Very often this special edition would be a limited edition. **Trade edition** in this context means 'ordinary edition', one for mass distribution.

The Limited Edition

The idea of the 'limited edition' has recently been subjected to much rough handling by the purveyors of bric-a-brac and the like in the pages of glossy magazines. The idea is exploited to suggest that the object in question will be of some value merely because it is made in 'limited numbers'. Would that this were true!

The fact is that *all* books are published in limited editions, in the sense that there is no such thing as an *un*limited edition - the printing has to stop sometime. **Limited edition** as used in the trade might be defined as an edition of which the number of copies printed is stated in each copy, though this definition is probably not watertight. The statement as to number of copies printed is known as the 'notice of limitation'. It may be found at any of several places in the book - on the verso of the title or the half-title, on a separate leaf, often somewhere at the end of the book. Very often this statement as to limitation is the *only* indication that the book is a limited edition - there may be nothing special about the paper on which the book is printed, the type used, or the binding of the book. And there may be no simultaneous trade edition with which to compare. Evelyn Waugh's *Work Suspended* was published in a limited editon of 500 copies in 1942. Nothing about the book suggests that it is in any way different from any other run-of-the-mill production.

However, 'limited edition' is often associated with 'fine edition', an edition on special paper, perhaps with a special typeface, with generous margins and a fine binding. Such an edition is frequently contrasted with a trade edition, but not always. There are limited editions which conform to the popular idea just sketched out but which constitute the only edition of the work.

If it did not have its origins in France, the limited edition has certainly found its fullest expression in that country, perhaps in reaction to the less than satisfactory quality of much ordinary French printing. The limitation notice of French books, almost always found at the back of the volume, will often fill half a page or more. There may be 10 copies printed on very luxurious paper and bound in the best of leathers; 50 copies printed on slightly less luxurious paper and bound in second best leather; 150 copies printed on merely fine paper, in a binding verging on the humdrum; 500 copies printed on pretty ordinary paper, in a very ordinary binding. The greatest number of 'limitations within the limitation' I have ever come across is eight, though I would not claim this as a record.

Frequently, though not necessarily, each individual copy will be numbered, by hand if the edition is very small, by stamp if very large. A typical limitation notice might run: 'Edition limited to 350 copies, of which this is number . . .'. However, it isn't at all unusual for copies to escape onto the market without being numbered.

The fact that the limited edition is in practice a relatively short-run edition, combined with the fact the intention is to produce something out of the ordinary, distinct from the mass, results in a large field upon which the publisher can exercise his idiosyncracy. The idea of the limited edition can be embroidered in many ways. A few copies may be **out of series**. Strictly, this expression refers to a few extra copies run off as a precaution against the possibility of damaged sheets or bindings. In practice, such copies often amount simply to an extra limitation and are distributed to the author's or publisher's intimates. Such copies may or may not be marked in some special way. Some copies may be distinguished by letters rather than numbers, with the implication that they comprise the very crème de la crème of the edition. Some copies may be signed by the author, editor or some other contibutor to the book. More tangibly, the limited edition might contain material additional to that in the trade edition, for example, if the book is illustrated, an extra set of the illustrations.

Nevertheless, many limited editions are fine examples of book production, books that are minor works of art in themselves and a pleasure to handle as well read. The time and money spent on their production often means that they are relatively expensive. The publisher may decide that he is likely to sell only a small number and therefore decides to produce only a small number, and that number will be 'limited'. If the book is being printed by hand it may well be that a high standard of work cannot be maintained over more than a small print run. Hence a decision to produce a limited edition. If the book is illustrated, the blocks from which the illustrations are printed may be subject to rapid wear, so only a small number of copies can be printed. All these are legitimate reasons for the production of a limited edition.

Less legitimate is the desire to imply scarcity and hence value. As I have already said, all editions are 'limited'. The print run of many books may not reach a thousand copies. A publisher who prints what would be the usual number of copies and adds to each a notice of limitation - 'Edition limited to 850 copies' - is usually just trying to persuade the purchaser that he is buying something which he is not, namely, a book that is either scarce at the time of publication or one that will rapidly become scarce in the course of time.

The same rule of thumb applies with the limited edition as with the first edition. If the book is desirable in the first place, of some literary or artistic merit, then the limitation may well make it more valuable than an equivalent trade edition. However, if the book has none of these qualities, the fact of the edition being limited will make no difference at to its desirability, or more accurately lack of same.

Proof Copies

A **proof copy** is a trial copy of the printed text used to check for printing and other errors. Modern proof copies are generally folded and sewn in the normal way but bound in plain paper wrappers, often brown, sometimes carrying details of the publication but often left plain. An 'uncorrected proof' is an unchecked proof copy while 'corrected proof' describes the checked version of the text.

In the nineteenth century proofs came in the form of long strips of paper, known as **galley proofs**

The intellectual interest of the proof copy may lie in the differences evident between it and the final version of the work. The corrections may include last-minute changes to the text by the author. In this case the proof copy may arguably represent an intermediate state of the text, some way between the manuscript and the final published version.

Proof copies of literary works, especially modern first editions, can have some value. In very general terms, if an author's work is collected then proof copies of the works will also be collected, though they won't necessarily be more valuable than ordinary first editions. Given what has already been said about priority, it might be thought that the proof copy would always be more valuable than the first edition since it precedes the first edition. However, the collector of modern firsts is primarily interested in the first *published* version of his or her author. Proof copies are not published copies of the work; they are intended merely for internal use. Thus the status of the proof copy is somewhat ambiguous.

Binding the Book

The binding of the book had its origin in the need to provide a protective cover for the printed pages. As such the binding is theoretically of secondary importance to the printed pages. Indeed, strictly speaking, the 'book' consists solely of the printed pages while the binding, though physically attached to the book, is conceptually quite distinct.

However, despite its humble origins it wasn't long before the binding of the book began to develop an importance of its own. In particular, the possibilities of decoration were soon perceived and book binding quickly became an art-form. From the very earliest jewelled bindings of the fifteenth century through to modern art-bindings exploiting such materials as stainless steel and plastic, the binding of the book has demanded to be treated as a subject in its own right.

The literature on the subject is vast, running into thousands of volumes. Collectors make a lifetime's study of the work of particular periods, or even the work of individual binders. There are booksellers who specialise in the supply of 'library furniture', that is, the supply to customers of rows of handsome leather-bound sets intended purely for display.

The primary purpose of the binding is to protect the book from unnecessary wear. As such it needs to be strong and resilient. The first bindings were made of wooden boards, which were already in use to protect manuscripts. Wood was gradually replaced by varieties of paste-board, that is, layers of coarse paper glued together.

(The term **board** has several meanings in booksellers' parlance, each of them related. In the most general sense it is used to describe the hard covers of any book, referring not only to the wood, paste-board or other material, but to any covering over that board - paper, cloth or leather. In this sense, ‘board’ is virtually synonymous with ‘cover’. In a second, more restricted sense, ‘board’ refers to the boards, often covered in paper, in which many books of the later eighteenth century were originally issued by the bookseller. From this is derived the expression **original boards**.)

From the beginnings of printing until the early nineteenth century by far the most common covering for the board was leather. Up until the late seventeenth century, the two most common types of leather used in binding were vellum (the untanned skin of the animal, usually calf) and calf (the tanned skin). By the beginning of the eighteenth century, vellum had fallen out of favour, largely on grounds of cost. This is not to say that it ceased to be used entirely, rather that it was used on a much more restricted scale, generally for more expensive books. Vellum enjoyed something of a revival in the late nineteenth and early twentieth centuries as a binding material for the limited edition illustrated books popular at the time. Morocco (the tanned skin of the goat) was introduced into England towards the end of the seventeenth century. From the second quarter of the nineteenth century, with the development of large-scale printing, most books were bound in cloth. (More will be said about leather bindings in the next chapter.)

The development of the cloth-bound book coincides roughly with the development of the publishing business as we know it, with one person or company commissioning the book and overseeing the whole process of publication. Prior to this, the publishing role would be undertaken by the printer or bookseller. However, the binder often worked quite independently of the printer/bookseller and the arrangements between the two could vary enormously. The printer might deliver the printed sheets to the binder with instructions merely to bind them at a certain price, leaving the binder to choose the materials. More often, particularly in the eighteenth century, the bookseller would deliver the sheets for a single copy of the book to a binder specified by the purchaser of the book. The binder would then bind the book according to the tastes of the purchaser.

As just mentioned, it was common practice, from the second half of the eighteenth century until the advent of cloth binding in the early nineteenth, for the bookseller to issue the book in a temporary binding of rough boards. The purchaser would buy the book in that form and take the book to his binder, who would then remove the boards and bind the book to the purchaser's instructions. In practice, many books issued in this way were left unaltered. Copies still in original boards are much sought after by collectors.

Strictly speaking, a book is *bound* only if the gatherings and the boards form a single structural unit. The gatherings are fastened together by means of sewing across tapes or cords which run at right angles to the backs of the gatherings, the ends of these tapes or cords then being let into holes in the boards and attached. When the covering material, usually leather, is placed over the boards it is generally glued to the back of the gatherings.

Virtually all leather-bound books up to the beginning of the nineteenth century are bound in this way. It follows that all such bindings are unique, since bespoke. The binding may be quite anonymous - a simple covering of undecorated calf. Often, though, the binding is quite distinctive and even, in a few cases, identifiable as the work of a particular binder. All this changes with the introduction of cloth binding, which coincides with the advent of mass production. From now on, the publisher will commission the binding of the book. All or most copies of a particular issue will have an identical binding. This is known as **edition binding**. Moreover, this binding is intended by the publisher as the permanent covering for the book, not something that the purchaser will remove and replace, though that practice did not die out over night.

Most books 'bound' in cloth are not bound in the strict sense just described, but **cased**. A separate case has been constructed, usually of stiff board covered in cloth. The case comprises both upper and lower cover as well as the spine, all in a single unit. The gatherings are sewn as for a leather-bound book, with tapes running at right angles across the backs of the gatherings. But the case is attached simply by gluing the tape ends to the inside of the boards. Thus the gatherings are attached only at the hinges. Often an additional piece of cloth, usually mull, is pasted across the backs of the gatherings and overlapping at each side. The mull is then pasted to the inside of the boards to provide a stronger hinge. Sometimes mull would be used on its own. without tapes. Tape ends and mull can usually be detected under the endpaper by sight or touch.

Though usually associated with books of the modern period, a similar technique was used in the earliest days of book production. Typically, a single piece of vellum might be used, without boards, folded around the book.

Some modern books, particularly of the cheaper kind, are not stitched at all, but simply glued together. The sheets are folded and gathered, clamped in a machine and the spine ground off and then glued into a case or into wrappers. Many modern paperbacks are produced in this way, when the binding is known as a **perfect binding**, a somewhat ironical description since it is a far from perfect method of binding. The book cannot naturally be opened flat and when any pressure is applied in the opening single leaves have a tendency to spring loose. The technique was also popular in the nineteenth century when it was employed for the binding of books printed on especially thick paper, paper which did not lend itself easily to folding in the normal way. In most cases, the rubber that was used as glue has perished, leaving behind a messy dry dust and all the leaves loose. This type of binding is popularly known as **gutta-percha** after the rubbery material used for gluing the whole together.

Despite the fore-going, most people, booksellers included, apply the words 'binding' and 'bound' indiscriminately to all the methods just outlined. There is no harm in this as long as the strict sense of the word is not forgotten.

A very common type of binding involves a combination of two different materials - leather and cloth, cloth and paper, leather and paper, or two different types of cloth. Such a binding would typically have the spine and corners in one material and the rest of the boards in another, in which case it is **half-bound** (not to be misunderstood as referring to a binding that is in some way incomplete). If the spine alone, without the corners, is in one material and the boards in a second, then it is described as **quarter-bound**. Hence such expressions as 'quarter sheep', 'half leather', 'quarter calf'. Frequently, only the material covering the spine and/or corners is mentioned, leaving the reader of the catalogue to guess the material on the boards. If the binding is described as simply 'calf' or 'cloth' then it is assumed that the binding is **full calf** or **full cloth**, etc.

Backstrip is a common synonym for spine, while the word 'back' or 'backed' occurs frequently in such descriptions as 'cloth-backed boards', ie., a book with the covers of board and the spine, or backstrip, in cloth.

The best way to familiarise oneself with the structure of different types of binding is to take a few books apart, dreadful though the thought may be to those for whom the book is a reverential object. Many secondhand bookshops have a quantity of broken calf lying neglected somewhere on a shelf or in boxes and offered at a nominal price. It would be worth buying a few old books of this sort and taking them to pieces, as an aid to understanding. (It would not be a good idea to attempt this exercise while browsing through the bookseller's stock, even though much of that stock might appear decrepit.)

A type of phrase that crops up frequently in booksellers' catalogues, and which might confuse, is '3 vols in 2' or '5 vols in 7'. These elliptical expressions mean, respectively, 'three volumes bound up in two volumes' and 'five volumes bound up in seven volumes'. They reveal a slight deficiency in the language, since two separate and distinct senses of 'volume' are being employed. There is, firstly, the conceptual sense of the word, meaning the divisions of the work as decided upon by the author, editor or publisher. In the second sense, the word simply refers to the physical object, the book. Thus, taking the second of the examples above, a work might have been divided by its editor or author into five volumes, corresponding to five distinct sections of the subject matter; but probably because the sections were of very unequal length, it was found more convenient to bind the book into seven separate physical volumes.

Books issued in paper covers are not strictly 'bound' at all. Nevertheless, such coverings for books need to be mentioned. Though the term 'paperback' is probably associated exclusively with twentieth-century book production, books were in fact issued in paper covers throughout the eighteenth and nineteenth centuries. They tended to be smaller and thinner, closer to pamphlets than books proper. Children's books and popular books selling at cheap prices were often issued in paper covers. Often the covers would be printed with the title of the work, some description of the contents and a small illustration. Various expressions are used to describe these paper covers, among them **printed wrappers**, **original wrappers** (**wraps**). Given the fragile nature of the covering, few books in wrappers have survived in reasonably good condition. Those that have can be highly prized by collectors.

(*Wrapper* used in this sense should not be confused with the dust-wrapper of the modern cloth-cased book. This should in any case be more properly called the 'dust-jacket'.)

Occasionally, especially with cheap books and pamphlets, the sections were not sewn together through the folds but through holes **stabbed** a little way in from the inner edge. This is a very crude form of binding, the only obvious advantage being speed of operation. Frequently, books that have been bound in this way are later rebound conventionally. The old stab marks, however, can never be disguised.

And **staples** were sometimes used in the nineteenth century as a substitute for sewing the sections. This too is a highly unsatisfactory method of binding, with the stapled sections usually just glued to the binding material and not sewn together. The result is that the sections have often come away and the whole book is loose. Worse, the staples have often left rust marks on the paper.

Marbled paper is a paper much used in book bindings of the seventeenth, eighteenth and nineteenth centuries, either as covering for the boards or as endpapers. It is highly coloured in a variety of fantastic abstract designs. Its manufacture requires a trough of gum over the surface of which coloured inks are sprinkled. The mutual repulsion of gum and ink ensures that the inks lie on the surface. The colours are then combined by almost any means that takes the maker's fancy - combing, stirring, brushing &c - until the pattern is achieved. The paper to be coloured is then let down gently onto the surface of the gum, the colours adhere to the paper, the paper is removed and then left to dry. The first European marbled papers were is use in Holland at the very end of the sixteenth century and they were introduced into England around the middle of the seventeenth century. In later years, particularly in England, the edges of the book might also be marbled. Modern so-called marbled paper found in art shops is almost always colour-printed by machine and has none of the feel of the hand-made product.

Leather Bindings

Many different types of animal skin (including human skin) have been used at one time or another to bind books. The skins most commonly used are those of the calf, the goat, the sheep and the pig, and this discussion will be limited to these four.

Vellum

Vellum is among the oldest forms of leather material used for binding. It is found on books of the early sixteenth century, and in England at least continued in general use until the second half of the seventeenth. It never completely died out but has tended to be used since then only for special editions.

The term does not refer to a type of skin but to a method of preparing the skin. Vellum is the *untanned* hide of the animal, usually calf, but possibly sheep or goat. Instead of being tanned, the hide is simply degreased, cleaned and treated with allum. The characteristic colour of a vellum binding is off-white or cheesy yellow. Vellum is a very hard wearing material. It is not at all uncommon to find sixteenth-century vellum bindings still in almost as good a condition today as when they were first put on the book. In the sixteenth century in particular vellum was often used on its own, intead of being laid over boards. This style of binding is known as **limp vellum**. While vellum could be dyed it was usually left in its 'natural' colour. It was occasionally decorated with gilt, but more usually left plain.

Calf

Calf is probably the most common type of leather binding. Unlike vellum, calf is the tanned hide of the animal. Calf was used from the very earliest days, especially on the Continent, when it would be laid over wooden boards.

Dyed calf bindings are to be found, but are not nearly as common as calf in its 'natural' brown colour. Other forms of decoration, however, were favoured. One method characteristic of eighteenth-century calf bindings involved staining the leather with acid, thereby producing a variety of effects. Four main decorative styles are distinguished: **marbled calf**, **sprinkled calf**, **mottled calf** and **tree calf**. The smooth surface of the skin could also be given a particular shine, hence **polished calf**.

Calf is a much less hard wearing skin than vellum, its comparative weakness stemming not least from the tanning process itself. A calf-bound book a century or more old is likely to show signs of wear along the hinges, as well as at the book's **extremities**, ie., the edges, corners and spine ends.

A variation on the ordinary calf binding found in the eighteenth and early nineteenth centuries, especially on what are generically termed 'family Bibles', is called **reversed calf**. This, as the name suggests, is the inner skin of the hide used as the outer surface of the binding. Reversed calf has a very distinctive feel to it, like suede. It can also be a rather unpleasant binding to handle, since often very friable and inclined to stain hands and clothing.

Russia is a variety of calf tanned by a special process and then oiled.

Morocco

Morocco is the term used to designate the hide of the goat, doubtless because the first leathers to be used in book binding, towards the end of the seventeenth century, were imported from North Africa. Morocco is almost always dyed, often in strong colours, from which it follows there is no characteristic morocco colour, as there is with both calf and vellum.

It is a comparatively hard wearing leather and most examples show a grain of some sort. The three most common types of morocco are firstly, **hard grain morocco** - a hard skin with a very noticeable close grain giving a pebbly effect; secondly **levant** - a rather loose-grained skin, often highly polished; thirdly, **niger** - the softest of all moroccos, with a variable, somewhat indeterminate grain. Confusingly, perhaps, 'levant' morocco originated in the Levant and 'niger' in West Africa.

Two common decorative effects involve modifying the grain of the leather. With **crushed morocco** the skin has been put in a press and the original tight grain enlarged or spread out. **Straight-grained morocco** is a skin that has had an artificial grain impressed into it, in the form of more or less parallel lines packed closely together.

Sheep

Sheep is generally a poor quality leather, typically brown in colour, like calf. It wears quickly, deteriorating along the spine and hinges. The surface of the skin is also susceptible to flaking and peeling. Its use tended to be confined to cheaper books - pocket books of verse, school text books and the like - from the sixteenth to the eighteenth centuries. It is seldom decorated, with at most a line or two ruled in blind (see below). **Roan** is a kind of sheep skin, very thin and not hard wearing.

Pig

Pig is the least common leather found in book binding, at least in England. (It was somewhat more popular on the Continent, particularly in the seventeenth and eighteenth centuries.) It is a very hard wearing leather, yellowish in colour when left untanned (like vellum) and distinguished by the appearance of a series of holes in the surface marking the place of the animal's hairs.

Decoration of Leather

Apart from the practice already mentioned of dying or staining leather, a variety of decorative effects are achieved by impressing a design or pattern into the leather by means of a tool.

Two distinct types of tooling are common: firstly, **blind-tooling**, in which the tool has been applied direct to the leather, leaving a plain impression in the surface, like embossing in reverse; secondly, **gilt-tooling**, in which a layer of gold leaf or cheaper substitute is first laid on the leather and the tool applied over it, leaving a gilt line or decoration impressed into the leather.

A great variety of terms are used to describe the different effects achieved by these two processes, and different booksellers may employ different terms to describe the same effect. Some booksellers will limit themselves to a very brief description of the decoration while others will describe it at length. Some books require an elaborate description, many perhaps fortunately, do not.

The words 'blind' and 'gilt' are frequently used without the accompanying word 'tooled' or 'tooling' ('covers elaborately gilt', 'spine gilt', 'upper board ruled in blind').

Stamped is sometimes used as a synonym for 'tooled'. However, 'stamped' strictly describes a process of impressing or moulding a design into the leather after it has been put on the book but before it has dried out. In practice, particularly with very early books, there may be no discernible difference in the end result of the two processes. But there could be no such thing as gilt-*stamped* decoration, since the damp leather would not take the gold leaf.

A **fillet** is a line ruled in the leather by means of a revolving wheel. Fillets can be single, double or triple; they may be plain (blind), more commonly they are gilt ('gilt fillet round cover').

A **panel** is a simple rectangular design on the covers formed by lines, or fillets ('contemporary panelled calf').

Dentelles - from the French word for lace - refers to a decorative pattern on the leather turned inside the covers. This pattern is usually 'lacy', hence the name.

A form of decoration usually found most commonly on calf bindings involves impressing a diamond, or lattice pattern across the entire board. This effect is known as **diced calf**.

The term **block** is occasionally used in the sense of 'tooled' ('covers blocked in gilt'). 'Block' generally implies that a more or less complex design, perhaps a crest or monogram, has been impressed into the leather with one engraved piece of metal.

Prize calf refers to the kind of leather binding typical of books given as prizes in schools or colleges, especially in the second half of the last century. The calf is usually polished or stained - marbled, tree calf &c - the spine is conventionally gilt, and on the upper board is impressed, or blocked, the arms of the institution concerned. It should be noted that many books in prize calf are in fact *cased*, after the fashion of cloth bindings, and not bound in the strict sense.

Inlays are separate pieces of leather, of a different colour, which have been let into the surface of the leather covering the board, to produce a pattern or illustration. **Onlays** are similar except that they have simply been stuck to the surface of the leather of the cover.

Decorating the Spine

If cords rather than tapes are used in the binding of the book they are often left standing proud at the back of the gatherings under the leather. They are then known as **raised bands** and have the effect of dividing the spine into **compartments**. The bookbinder frequently makes a virtue of necessity by making a decorative feature of what otherwise might be considered a rather ugly aspect of the spine. The raised bands might themselves have a gilt rule across them; very often, the compartments into which they divide the spine are themselves decorated, perhaps with lines or rules, perhaps with some sort of design or motif. The term 'device', already met with in the context of 'printer's device' is used by some booksellers to refer to such a design.

Raised bands quickly came to be viewed as a 'traditional' part of the binding, to the point where binders would sometimes make fake raised bands in the spine, that is, bands not corresponding to any cords underneath. Sometimes a book without raised bands would nevertheless have gilt lines across the spine in an echo of the band.

The spine also carries details of the book's title, perhaps the author and details of any volume number. With leather-bound books these details are frequently found on a **lettering piece** or a **label**, that is, a small section of leather which is glued onto the spine, in one of the compartments. This section of leather is usually of morocco and often of a different colour to that of the binding. In the early years of the nineteenth century these lettering pieces were occasionally made of paper.

If no lettering piece is employed, and the details of title etc are tooled straight onto the spine, then the spine is described as **lettered direct**.

Decorating the Edges

The edges of the book are also often decorated, most commonly with a layer of gilt. **All edges gilt** (abbreviated to **a.e.g.**) indicates that all three edges - top, bottom and fore - have been treated this way. **Top edge gilt** (**t.e.g.**) indicates that the top edge only had been gilded. While largely decorative in purpose, the gilding on the top edge at least does serve a practical purpose, in as much as it helps to prevent dust from penetrating between the leaves. Occasionally the edges of the book might be gilded *before* sewing; when the book came to be sewn and bound, these edges would not be trimmed smooth in the normal way. These uncut gilded edges are known as **gilt on the rough**.

Another form of decoration involves impressing a design into the edges to produce an embossed effect. This effect is known as **gauffred edges**). Gauffred edges are almost always gilt as well.

A sought-after decorative feature of the fore-edge is the **fore-edge painting**, a painting executed on the fore-edge of the book while the leaves are fanned out. The fore-edge is afterwards gilded, with the result that the painting is invisible when the book is closed. Only by fanning out the leaves can the picture be seen. Fore-edge paintings vary enormously in quality and interest. They were popular in England in the eighteenth and early nineteenth centuries, especially on small books of verse, gift books, small Bibles and prayer books and the like. Many fore-edge paintings are of dubious provenance; many are still being produced today. Even the most thorough of booksellers will occasionally fail to check every little gilt-edged book of the period that comes his way; once in a very long while, a fore-edge painting goes unnoticed, and the lucky purchaser can generally look forward to a large profit.

The Age of the Binding

A variety of terms are used to indicate the age of a leather binding or, to put the point another way, when the binding was put on the book.

As I have already pointed out, prior to the introduction of cloth as a binding material in the early nineteenth century it was the custom for the purchaser of the book to organise the binding of the book himself. The book would be purchased either in sheets or in some form of temporary binding, such as rough boards, and then be given to the purchaser's own binder who would bind it to the customer's instructions. This practice was extremely common; probably the majority of leather-bound books were bound in this way. A variation of this practice involved the bookseller organising the binding himself, perhaps with an 'in-house' binder, but still to the customer's specifications.

Sometimes the bookseller would organise the binding of a number of copies himself, particularly when he thought there was a ready sale for them, or demand would be strong; or when the book was of a particularly topical or ephemeral nature. We can conjecture that cheap publications such as school text books would sometimes be bound up directly by the bookseller and offered bound to the public. However, in most cases, we can't be sure, if only because few records survive. And undoubtedly there were occasions when a bookseller offered for sale copies of more substantial works ready bound. The difficulty lies in distinguishing them from copies not sold in this way.

In these circumstances, it is, in my opinion, very difficult to apply the word 'original' when describing the binding nowadays, given that the word strictly designates any feature of the book present *when the book was first issued to the public by the publisher*, and excludes any feature added later by a subsequent owner. Some leather-bound books still circulating are probably in 'original calf'; the difficulty lies in distinguishing them from the majority which aren't. Given the near impossibility of making any such distinction in the majority of cases, in my opinion it is better to avoid the use of 'original' altogether in the context of pre-1800 leather bindings, though some booksellers might disagree. Eschewing 'original', the word used to describe a leather binding put on the book at or about the time of publication is **contemporary** ('contemporary morocco', 'contemporary half calf').

'Later' suggests that the current binding - the book may after all have been rebound at some time in its life - was put on some time after the book's publication, too far from the time of publication to be 'contemporary' but still sufficiently removed from the present as not to be 'recent'. 'Recent' suggests a binding put on in perhaps the last two or three decades, though different booksellers will have different interpretations of the term. 'Modern' describes a binding put on in the last year or two, possibly by the bookseller who is offering the item for sale. Finally, 'old' is the least definitive of descriptions; the binding may or may not be contemporary, but it isn't recent or modern. Further than that, the bookseller is not prepared to commit himself.

Rebinding

The older the binding the more likely it is to have been repaired or restored at some time in its life. I have already mentioned 'recent' and 'modern', terms which imply that the old binding has been replaced. Often parts of the old binding have been preserved, especially if the main areas of wear are along the joints. If a book has been **rebacked** we understand that a new spine has been put on the book but that the old boards have been retained. If the old spine is still in reasonably good condition, and if it can be removed cleanly, it is often glued back onto the piece of leather which has been used to make a new spine. This would be described as 'rebacked retaining original spine'.

Rebound implies that the whole binding has been replaced, with the further implication that the rebinding is recent.

Cloth Bindings

When looking at cloth bindings we are interested primarily in the question of who was responsible for putting the binding on the book and only slightly in the particular material used. Many of the descriptive terms used with reference to cloth bindings refer to the circumstances of binding rather than the material. Most book cloths are varieties of linen. **Buckram**, the only cloth commonly distinguished by name, is a particularly coarse linen stiffened with gum. 'Publisher's cloth' refers not to a type of cloth but to a cloth binding which has been put on the book by the publisher. Much work has been done investigating the varieties of cloth used in book binding, especially in the nineteenth century. Some of this work is highly technical, and among other things has resulted in the production of a classification system for colours of cloth. Cloths of the nineteenth century in particular are often textured. Some cloths are *ribbed*, strongly or faintly; others have a *grain* imparted to them: sand-grain, diaper-grain, fine-grain, bubble-grain, etc. While a technical knowledge of the different types of cloth and the methods used to process them is of slight importance to most collectors and dealers, anyone with a particular interest in the nineteenth century would be advised to make a study of specialist catalogues and bibliographies to familiarise him or herself with the terms employed to distinguish textures and colours, since so much depends on variations between such things, especially when distinguishing between editions and issues.

The search for a suitable cloth for binding purposes extended over a period of several decades in the early nineteenth century. The cloth had to be fairly hard wearing, able to take glue without staining and capable of being stretched over the case without wrinkling or other distortion. The discovery of the first cloth suitable for binding is attributed to one William Pickering, a bookseller and publisher, and the first cloth bindings began to appear in quantity in the 1820's. This early cloth was an unattractive thing by our standards, rather coarse in texture, dull of colour and generally unadorned. At most there might be a rule or two in blind; the spine might carry a printed paper label with details of the work. The one significant merit of these early cloths is that they proved to be very hard wearing; they are often found today in almost as good a state as when they were first put on the book.

From the 1820's onwards the development of book cloth proceeded apace until by the middle of the century we find much more sophisticated bindings - cloths of smoother texture, dyed in a variety of colours and, perhaps most importantly, capable of taking gold leaf as decoration. As new materials and techniques were discovered so publishers were quick to exploit them in an attempt to make the book more attractive to the potential customer. The binding had become a 'selling point' in our jargon.

It is at this point that we can begin to speak with confidence of **publisher's cloth**, a cloth binding that is, firstly, identifiably the responsibility of the publisher of the book; secondly, intended as a permanent binding for the book; and thirdly, a binding common to all copies of the book issued at one time. **Original cloth** is often used as a synonym for publisher's cloth. By contrast with attempts to apply the word 'original' to leather bindings of the eighteenth century and earlier, 'original' applied to cloth refers precisely to a binding which is identifiable as the product of the publisher.

'Publisher's binding' is not quite synonymous with 'publisher's cloth'. In practice, the great majority of publisher's bindings are of cloth and to that extent the two terms are interchangeable. However, **publisher's leather** is also occasionally met with. In most cases, publisher's leather is simply an adaptation of the cloth case. Instead of the case being made entirely out of cloth, a leather spine and corners might be added; the whole would then be described, somewhat pedantically, as 'publisher's half-leather case'.

There is an enormous variety of styles in cloth decoration, particularly from about the 1850's to the 1900's, involving stamping, printing, embossing, or a combination of all three. (Some of the terms already discussed in the context of leather bindings apply equally to cloth.) Cloth and printed paper are sometimes used together; sometimes the upper board (the front cover of the book) is made up of two different pieces laid one on top of the other, with the central portion of the upper board cut away to create a recess effect with an illustration or photograph let in. Towards the end of the nineteenth century and into the twentieth, cloths carrying a picture in colour were used, especially for the works of the more popular novelists as well as for what are loosely termed 'boys' books', the novels, for example, of W.H.G. Kingston and G.A. Henty. Kipling's novels were frequently issued in a blue cloth with a quite elaborate design blocked in gold on the upper board.

Despite this variety, the two terms most commonly used in the description of cloth are fairly imprecise. **Decorated cloth** can mean any sort of cloth with any sort of decoration. **Pictorial cloth** means any sort of cloth with an illustration on the upper board at least, possibly on both boards and the spine. The looseness of the terms derives not least from the fact that a binding may be both decorative and pictorial, in which case either term may be used with equal effect. Unless the contrary is stated, both pictorial cloth and decorated cloth will also be publisher's cloth.

'Edition binding', as we have seen, indicates that all or most copies of a given issue of a book have an identical binding. Various types of cloth binding fall outside this category, the most common being **binder's cloth**. The strict definition of 'binder's cloth' is any cloth that is unique to the particular copy (as opposed to edition binding). For many booksellers the term also implies a rebinding, ie., a replacement binding. In practice, 'binder's cloth' is used much more loosely. Binder's cloth is generally distinguished by its rather rough and ready nature, a coarse cloth dull of colour with either no decoration at all or a bare minimum. In appearance it approximates closely to the early cloth bindings of the 1820's and 1830's already described. And indeed, while those early bindings were often the responsibility of the publisher, since they have few of the characteristics of publisher's cloth they are sometimes, somewhat inaccurately, described as being of binder's cloth. More generally, and more loosely still, 'binder's cloth' implies a series of negatives: a binding not put on by the publisher, not put on at the time of issue, a binding not shared by other copies of the book, and a binding not at all attractive.

Library cloth may be understood as a variety of binder's cloth, in the strict sense of that term, that is, a binding unique to a particular copy. In appearance, library cloth is frequently so similar to binder's cloth as to be indistinguishable. What does distinguish the two is that a binding of library cloth is identifiable as a binding put on the book by a library. In other words, a given institution has bought a copy of the book, had the original binding removed and replaced, usually by something more durable than the original. A book thus rebound will almost certainly have markings inside as a pointer to its provenance.

An important institution of the nineteenth century was the circulating library, a business which offered subscribers the opportunity to borrow books from its stock. It was often the practice of such libraries to buy copies of a book - several at least, possibly substantially more depending on their subscription list and the estimated demand for the title - direct from the publisher in sheets, ie., unbound. The libraries would then have the copies bound to their own specifications. The description 'library cloth' is generally reserved for a binding put on a book by an institutional library and not a commercial lending library. The latter type of binding might be described as binder's cloth.

A not uncommon practice in the early years of the nineteenth century was for the publisher/printer to sell quantities of the sheets of the same book to various middlemen, perhaps in different parts of the country, who would then have them bound and sell them wholesale to the bookshops. Such bindings are known as **distributor's bindings** and are often confused with publisher's bindings.

A further complication with cloth bindings stems from the fact that publishers would often bind only a portion of the total print run at any one time. A publisher might have printed, for example, 1,000 copies of a given work. (Economies of scale dictate that the difference in cost between printing 1,000 copies and 500 copies is not great.) However, if the venture was at all speculative - the first work of a new writer, or one of uncertain reputation - the publisher might decide to have only 400 copies bound initially, to gauge the demand. When those 400 copies had been sold, the publisher would order another quantity to be bound. But this might be after an interval of a few weeks or months, by which time the binder no longer had in stock the same cloth used for the first batch. Thus the second batch would have a different cloth, and perhaps also different decoration. When this second batch was exhausted, a third batch would be bound up, in yet another type of cloth, and so on. It isn't unusual for bibliographers to discover half a dozen or more different bindings on what are all copies of the same edition of a work. An extreme example of this is George Borrow's *Lavengro* (1851) for which some nine different bindings have been identified all on copies of the first edition.

As long as it can be established that these bindings were all put on by the publisher then they are all correctly described as 'publisher's cloth'. Whether they are also correctly described as 'original cloth' is perhaps moot. What is not moot at all is the fact that a second or subsequent binding would constitute a **secondary binding** or a **variant binding**, and as such would generally be of somewhat less interest to the collector, who puts a premium on priority. The description of a binding as 'secondary' or 'variant' presupposes, of course, that bibliographical research has determined priority. Where priority has not been established the collector faced with several different bindings on the same book can only collect them all, consoling himself with the thought that one among them is the 'first issue binding' even if he doesn't know which one it is.

As if matters weren't complicated enough, a further complication needs to be mentioned (a further and final one in this book at least, the reader may be pleased to know). The publisher may have decided, after binding perhaps two-thirds of a print run, that he had no use for the remaining sheets and just wanted rid of them. Rather than pulp them he might have 'remaindered' them, that is, sold them cheaply to another publisher or bookseller, who would have had them bound and then sold them on, still at a low price. This practice accounts for the existence of the **remainder binding**. A remainder binding may, in point of appearance, resemble binder's cloth at one extreme or publisher's cloth at the other. (The practice of remaindering is still, of course, prevalent today - some might say too prevalent - though what is remaindered is the whole book, already bound.)

At the beginning of this chapter I remarked that, with regard to cloth bindings, the important question demanding an answer is, Who put the binding on the book? The question might be expanded slightly by adding, When? and, Under what circumstances? We have looked at some of the possible answers to these questions. These questions are of importance primarily for those interested in publishing of the nineteenth century. (Prior to that time the questions would not arise since there were no cloth bindings; after the nineteenth century, though many of the points raised in this chapter still apply, in practice binding procedures had become much more stabilised and standardised.) The great variety of binding styles and practices of the nineteenth century reflect in part the huge growth in publishing of the time, a wide-spread entrepreneurial spirit among publishers large and small, all vying with each other to take advantage of the demand for books as well as creating demand for different types of literature. For the person with scant interest in the period, persuing the ramifications of binding practice may well be tedious. For the person who is fascinated by the nineteenth century, hunting for the explanations of differences in bindings can throw light not only on the bindings themselves but on the history of a particular book's publication, even its writing; on the relations between author and publisher, perhaps on the life of the author himself.

The Dust-Jacket

The **dust-jacket**, or **dust-wrapper** (abbreviated to **d.j.** and **d.w.**), has probably provoked more controversy among book collectors in the course of its relatively short life than almost any other part of the book. For collectors of modern first editions in particular, the presence or absence of the dust-jacket can make the difference between a copy that is worth hundreds of pounds and one that is worth merely tens. Not only must the jacket be present, it should preferably be in pristine condition as well. A familiar sight in book shops and at fairs is that of the dealer in modern first editions carefully examining the *inside* of the dust-jacket, as well as the outside, for the slightest blemish.

Many book buyers and collectors of pre-war days, by contrast, considered the dust-jacket an unmitigated nuisance and discarded it as soon as they got the book home. There was outright resentment at being forced to buy what was deemed a superfluous piece of packaging, one whose cost presumably inflated the purchase price of the book. A publisher in 1935 referred to the dust-jacket as "that wretched thing, of which we sometimes deplore the very existence". At the British Museum library, the book jackets were stored separately from the books; when storage space was at a premium, the jackets were thrown out. It is this attititude to the dust-jacket as much as general wear and tear which accounts for the present-day scarcity of jackets of the 1920's, 30's and 40's.

At issue is the question of whether the dust-jacket should be considered an integral part of the book. In its earliest days the jacket was not so considered and hence was often discarded. Latterly, opinion among collectors at least has swung round to the opposite position with the result that the packaging has become as prized as the product, and frequently much more valuable. Notwithstanding that, there are still those today, readers rather than collectors, who treat the jacket with disdain and throw it away as soon as it shows signs of wear.

The history of the dust-jacket is closely allied to the history of the cloth-bound book. In origin, the jacket was intended as a temporary protective covering for the cloth covers while the book was on the shelves of the bookseller. Even then, publisher's cloth bindings had been in existence for many years before the dust-jacket became a standard feature of the book.

A serious obstacle to elucidating the history of the dust-jacket is the fact that so few of the early examples have survived to the present day. Dust-jackets of the nineteenth century, in particular, are exceptionally rare. The earliest known dust-jackets date from the 1830's. They consisted of a one-colour piece of rather flimsy paper, usually with the title of the work printed on the upper panel and often details of other works by the same author or from the same publisher on the lower panel.

By the 1850's some publishers were using plain transparent **glassine wrappers**, through which the design of the covers could be seen. This form of jacket was particularly popular with publishers of **yellow backs**, cheap reprints of popular novels in paper-covered boards. The upper board would have some lurid picture illustrating a scene from the book printed on it, usually against a background of garish yellow. Since this decorated binding was a strong selling point, it would make no sense at all to hide it. Hence the use of a transparent wrapper. Nowadays, of course, the position is exactly the reverse, with all the effort to catch the eye being put into the design of the jacket.

Glassine jackets remained in use up until the end of the nineteenth century. Many of Rudyard Kipling's works of the 1880's and 1890's were issued with glassine wrappers and they are still occasionally found today, though usually much torn and soiled.

The printed dust-jacket, as opposed to the pictorial or decorative, was used intermittently by publishers throughout the latter half of the nineteenth century and into the twentieth. Typical examples can be found on copies of the *Highways and Byways* series of topographical books issued by Macmillan in the 1900's. Lewis Carroll's *Hunting of the Snark* (1876) carried a printed dust-jacket, though copies with the jacket are very rare.

It was not until the turn of the century that the decorative dust-jacket as we know it began to come into fashion. One of the earliest examples is found on another of Kipling's works, *The Just So Stories* (1902). The history of the dust-jacket in England in the first two decades of the twentieth century is that of, generally, more or less crude illustration on the upper panel and printed publicity material, either for the publisher or for some commercial concern, on the lower. Publishers, particularly of popular fiction, were beginning to realise the possibilities of the dust-jacket as a selling point for the book but were still not prepared to devote many resources to them.

By the late 1920's the situation had changed quite dramatically, at least with regard to fiction. The decorated dust-jacket had come into its own, often at the expense of the cloth cover. The effort that for many years had gone into decorating the covers of the book was now transferred to the jacket. In the decade or so before the Second World War artists of the stature of William Orpen and Frank Brangwyn designed jackets, while Evelyn Waugh, already a designer of jackets before he turned to writing, was responsible for the jackets of several of his own novels.

The 1940's and 1950's mark for some the high-point in British dust-jacket design, the period in which it might be said to constitute a minor art form in its own right. Artists such as Graham Sutherland, John Piper, Duncan Grant, Barnett Freidmann and Edward Ardizzone all produced designs for jackets, as well as figures as diverse as Cecil Beaton, Mervyn Peake and Len Deighton. In addition to these well-known names there were a number of minor figures, unknown to the general public, devoting themselves to jacket design. The series of books published around this time by Batsford based loosely on the theme of England's heritage is much collected, and one of the main attractions of these books are the dust-jackets designed by Brian Cook.

For anyone interested in the 'art of the book', dust-jackets of this period might well prove an interesting collecting field. To my knowledge, it is as yet almost completely negelected. The books themselves, in large part novels of the time by authors now completely forgotten, can often be found very cheaply and a visit to most secondhand bookshops is likely to yield something of interest.

The importance of the dust-jacket to the collector has already been stressed. But the jacket is important not only to the collector of modern first editions. Almost any book originally issued in a dust-jacket, regardless of the subject matter, will be worth somewhat more if the jacket is still present and in reasonably good condition.

Such is the importance of the dust-jacket to collectors of modern first editions, however, there is now a trade in the jackets alone. And theft of the jacket, without the book, is a growing problem for booksellers. An important consideration in this trade is whether the dust-jacket matches the book. The specialist bookseller removes the jacket not only to examine the state of the jacket itself but also to check on the condition of the covers. A fine-condition jacket over covers that are dull and rubbed will suggest that the book has existed for some time without a jacket, even that the present jacket was taken from another copy. This mis-matching can devalue the book quite considerably.

I once bought a large collection of books from a rather eccentric individual who had been in the habit of removing the dust-jackets, folding them, then placing them inside the covers of the book. (He evidently could not make up his mind whether the jackets should be discarded or not, so he compromised.) Among his collection were many first editions of books by such authors as Grahame Greene, George Orwell, Anthony Powell and W.H. Auden. The covers themselves had all lost that freshness characteristic of covers that have been protected, while the jackets, though a little creased, were mostly in very good condition. Having replaced the jackets on the books I then had the problem of explaining to customers that, despite appearances, the jackets were in fact original to the books.

A final point worth mentioning concerns Penguin paperbacks. Many early Penguins were originally issued with a dust-jacket, though the idea of a dust-jacketed paperback may seem strange to us. In most cases, the design of the jacket replicated the design of the upper panel of the wrapper itself.

Signatures, Inscriptions and Annotations

One of the more confusing aspects of book collecting, particularly with reference to value, concerns evidence of previous ownership, in the form of an owner's name, an inscription, underlining, notes or whatever. More than once I have been asked, more or less plaintively, "But *why* isn't the book worth anything? The author's signed it, hasn't he?" The presence of the author's signature has assumed a mystique for the layperson, aided no doubt by the fashion for 'signing sessions' at new bookshops. The old joke among hardened sceptics of the trade is that an *unsigned* copy of the memoirs of the latest politician or celebrity is probably more valuable than a signed copy, given the scarcity of the former. The fact is that signatures, inscriptions and annotations *may* add to the value of the book, though they are as likely to detract from the value. Three criteria may be applied when coming to a decision. Firstly, to what extent do the marks affect the visual appeal of the book? How extensive are they? How obtrusive? How far in keeping with the book (contemporary with publication or much later)? Where do they appear? (on the endpapers, on the title, in the body of the book)? Secondly, what is the significance, if any, of the marks? Do they add to the interest to the book? Are they by someone of importance, (the author himelf or a subsequent owner)? Thirdly, what is the intrinsic value of the book, independently of any marks?

In many cases the presence of an ownership mark will neither add to nor subtract from the value of a book. Indeed, it is standard practice among catalogue booksellers to ignore all 'minor inscriptions', at least with the cheaper book. The most common type of mark is a previous **owner's name**, sometimes with a date. On the endpaper of the book, this can usually be ignored. If it appears on the half-title or title-page, attention should be drawn to it. If the mark is in some way out of keeping with the book (red ball-point scrawl in a seventeenth-century work) it will almost certainly reduce the book's value.

'Owner's name' must be distinguished from 'signature' or 'signed'. The use of either of the latter terms, without qualification, generally implies the signature of the author him or herself. A **signed copy** is a copy which bears the author's signature, a specific meaning unknown to a man who once tried to sell me a 'signed copy' of the bible. I presume he meant a copy which bore an *owner's name*. Signed copies of a book may be more valuable than unsigned copies, but not necessarily. The principle to apply in all cases is, does the book have value independently of the author's signature? If the answer is, yes, then the signature may add to the value, modestly or greatly. (A copy of a standard nineteenth-century work of scholarship, with an established value, may well attract a small premium if it has the author's signature. A desirable modern first edition with the author's signature will often attract a considerable premium.) Conversely, if the book is not in demand in the first place, the presence of the author's signature is not going to make it valuable, which is the answer to the question posed in the first paragraph.

Another aspect of the question serves to introduce the idea of **provenance**, that is, those hands the book has been through in the past. In practice, all secondhand books, by definition, have been through someone else's hands but this prior possession is generally only elevated to the status of provenance in cases where the previous owner was someone of note, or noteriety. An otherwise undistinguished book will be of some value if it bears the signature of Isaac Newton, Hermann Goerring or Henry Miller. Likewise, the young Thomas Carlyle's copy of a Latin grammar; or James Joyce's copy of a Dublin street map.

Allied to the idea of provenance is the **association copy**, a copy of a book interesting and valuable because of its association with someone of importance. This association may take the form of a signature or inscription; it may equally derive from prior possession by a library or private collection, often marked by a bookplate.

An **inscription** is something more extensive and elaborate than a mere signature. Typically it might consist of a few lines presenting the book from one person to another. The same principles apply as with the owner's name: is the inscription unsightly? in keeping with the book? where does it appear?

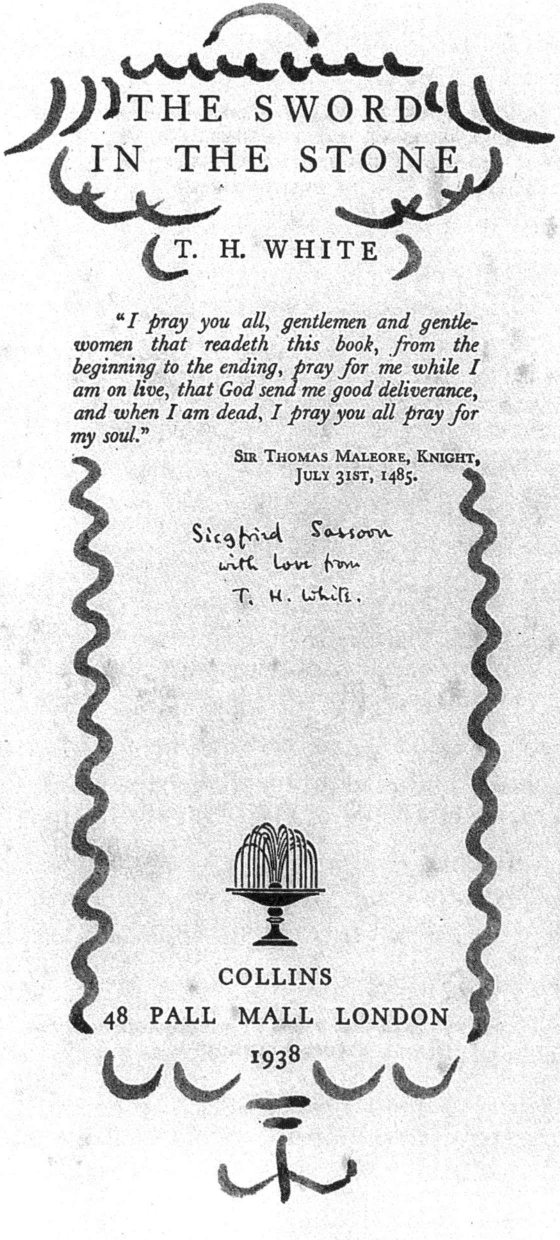

THE SWORD IN THE STONE

T. H. WHITE

"I pray you all, gentlemen and gentlewomen that readeth this book, from the beginning to the ending, pray for me while I am on live, that God send me good deliverance, and when I am dead, I pray you all pray for my soul."

SIR THOMAS MALEORE, KNIGHT,
JULY 31ST, 1485.

Siegfried Sassoon
with love from
T. H. White.

COLLINS
48 PALL MALL LONDON
1938

Presentation copy by T.H. White of one of his books to Siegfried Sassoon, one of six copies only personally decorated and signed by White for his friends.

'Owner's inscription' is distinguished from 'inscription' or 'inscribed'. An **inscribed copy**, without qualification, is taken to mean a copy bearing an inscription by the author, usually presenting the copy to someone. An alternative, more explicit expression is **signed presentation copy** (**s.p.c.**). As far as value is concerned, the same rule applies as with the signature: a desirable book will be made more desirable if it is a signed presentation copy, whereas an unwanted book will remain unwanted.

(In the manner of philosophers imagining extreme hypotheses to illustrate their thesis, one might construct a case to disprove the last assertion, involving provenance again. A man wrote a book on brick-laying and knowing Winston Churchill's interest in the subject, sent him a copy with a presentation inscription. Churchill material being much in demand among collectors, the question is, would this copy have any value? If there were signs that Churchill had perused it, better still, if he had annotated it, it would certainly have value. Otherwise the point would remain decidedly moot.)

The value of inscribed copies is often not easy to determine since, in the nature of things, they are unique. Some authors, particularly modern novelists, are in the habit of presenting many copies of their works to friends, thus inscribed copies of their books are relatively common and in some cases not much more valuable than unsigned copies. What might be termed the 'quality' of the inscription counts for a great deal. Briefly, the more interesting the inscription, the more valuable the copy. For example, Grahame Greene's signature in a first edition of one of his books would add to the copy's value; an inscription from Greene presenting the copy to someone unknown would add more value; a copy inscribed to a known friend would be more valuable still; a copy inscribed, say, to Evelyn Waugh would be extremely valuable indeed.

A variation of the inscribed copy which the collector needs to treat with some caution is the copy which is inscribed 'from the author' or 'with the author's compliments' but without an actual signature. Such inscriptions *may* be in the author's own hand, but not necessarily. It was not unknown, particularly in the nineteenth century, for the publisher of a book to detail one of the office clerks to write such an inscription in complimentary copies of the book before they were despatched.

Another form of ownership mark are marginal notes or comments. **Annotations** is the term most commonly used to cover all such marks.

Booksellers specialising in older books will sometimes refer to **marginalia**. Any attempt to lay down specific rules for the appraisal of books with annotations is bound to be difficult, since their variety and quality will vary enormously and in the end appraisal is in some ways subjective. In very general terms, the same criteria apply as have already been cited with regard to ownership marks and the like: are the annotations obtrusive and aesthetically unpleasing, or the reverse?, are they contemporary with the publication of the book, or not?, are they of some interest (did the annotator have something worthwhile to say)? are the annotations by someone of importance in their own right (perhaps by someone with specialist knowledge of the subject)? An assessment of the degree to which annotations affect value involves a balancing of all these considerations.

Marginal notes in older books, perhaps seventeenth century or earlier, can, if they are neatly executed and still legible, add to the interest of a copy if not to its value, even though the annotator may be anonymous. They bring home to today's collector the fact that the very copy he or she is now handling was once handled and perused by someone living three centuries or more ago. There are those who find this 'personalisation' of a copy attractive. In an attempt to convey the age of annotations booksellers will sometimes describe them as being in an **old hand** or in a **contemporary hand**.

As with signatures and inscriptions, annotations by a famous owner can often add value, or even *create* value where none was before (John Milton's copy of the *Eikon Basilike* with his annotations).

Book Illustration

Techniques for printing illustrations for books fall into three main categories: firstly, printing from the raised surface of a block of material which has been cut; secondly, printing from the incised parts of a sheet of material which has been cut; thirdly, printing from the flat surface of an uncut block or sheet of material.

Relief Printing

Printing from the raised surface of a block which has been cut is called **relief printing**. The most common material used in this kind of printing is wood (a block of wood, hence the term **block** which is sometimes met with in this connection). The most common woods employed are pear, apple and beech. The engraver works along the length of the grain, cutting the design out of the wood. In other words, the parts of the wood which are *not* going to print are cut away. The principle will be familiar to any one who has made potato prints, in adult or juvenile life. The potato is sliced in half and a design cut into the flat surface. The cut surface is dabbed in ink or paint and then stamped onto paper. The fact that the wood is *cut* gives rise to the term **wood-cut** to describe this technique and, by extension, the finished product ('wood-cut illustrations'). 'Wood-block' is occasionally used as a synonym for 'wood-cut'.

The block-book, already mentioned in the opening chapter, was an early form of primitive printing, consisting of an illustration and a few lines of text all cut from the one block of wood. The technical term for this technique is **xylography**. The block-book was in effect a kind of picture book, with the illustrated portion frequently coloured by hand after printing.

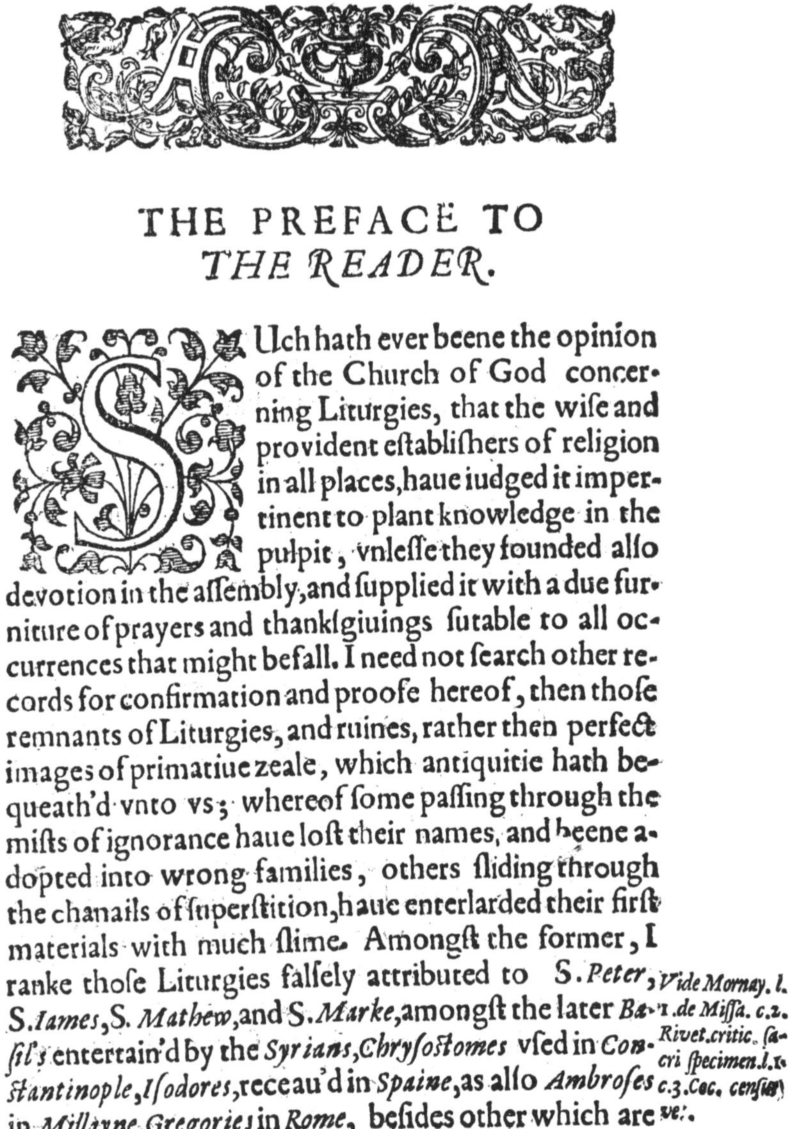

THE PREFACE TO
THE READER.

SUch hath ever beene the opinion of the Church of God concerning Liturgies, that the wiſe and provident eſtabliſhers of religion in all places, haue iudged it impertinent to plant knowledge in the pulpit, vnleſſe they founded alſo devotion in the aſſembly, and ſupplied it with a due furniture of prayers and thankſgiuings ſutable to all occurrences that might befall. I need not ſearch other records for confirmation and proofe hereof, then thoſe remnants of Liturgies, and ruines, rather then perfect images of primatiue zeale, which antiquitie hath bequeath'd vnto vs; whereof ſome paſſing through the miſts of ignorance haue loſt their names, and beene adopted into wrong families, others ſliding through the chanails of ſuperſtition, haue enterlarded their firſt materials with much ſlime. Amongſt the former, I ranke thoſe Liturgies falſely attributed to S. *Peter*, S. *Iames*, S. *Mathew*, and S. *Marke*, amongſt the later *Baſil's* entertain'd by the *Syrians*, *Chryſoſtomes* vſed in *Conſtantinople*, *Iſodores*, receau'd in *Spaine*, as alſo *Ambroſes* in *Millayne*, *Gregories* in *Rome*, beſides other which are

Vide Mornay. l. 1. de Miſſa. c.2. Rivet. critic. ſacri ſpecimen. l. 1. c.3. Coc. cenſura vet.

¶ 2 recounted

Wood-cut initial letter and head-piece from an early seventeenth-century work.

SECT. III.

ANGER.

As the whirlwind in its fury teareth up trees, and deformeth the face of nature; or as an earthquake in its convulsions overturneth whole cities; so the rage of an angry man throweth mischief around him. Danger and destruction wait on his hand.

But consider, and forget not thine own weakness; so shalt thou pardon the failings of others.

Wood-cut illustration from an edition of Robert Dodsley's "The Economy of Human Life", 1808, typical of wood-cuts 'in the text'.

A

GARLAND

OF

NEW SONGS.

The Country Club
The Chandler's Shop
Paddy M' Shane's Seven Ages.

Newcaſtle upon Tyne :
Printed by J. Marſhall, in the Old Fleſh-Market.
Where may alſo be had, a large and curious Aſſortment of Songs, Ballads, Tales, Hiſtories, &c.

Title-page of a popular song-sheet of the early nineteenth century, with a wood-cut illustration.

Two advantages of wood as a material are, firstly, that it is readily available, and secondly, that it is easy to work. Two main disadvantages stem from the softness of the material: firstly, except in the hands of expert craftsmen it is not usually possible to produce a design of any great sophistication; secondly, the finished block tends to wear quite quickly during printing, thus making long print runs difficult. This second disadvantage was overcome in the nineteenth century by making stereotype or electrotype blocks in metal from the original wooden blocks and printing from them. In particular, this technique allowed the wood-cut to be used in long-run magazines and periodicals, and it continued to be employed in this way well into the 1880's.

A third, very important advantage of the wood-cut technique stems from the fact that the block prints in relief, that is, from a raised surface. Printing from ordinary type is also a form of relief printing. This meant that a printer could set up a block of type and a wood-block together and print from them both in one operation, thereby saving time and effort. It is this particular advantage which explains why the typical wood-cut illustration is found 'in the text', that is, on the same page as a portion of text. Indeed, when booksellers refer to 'illustrations in the text' or 'text illustrations', without further comment, it is almost certain that the illustrations will be wood-cuts. Some, perhaps the more old-fashioned, will refer to **text cuts** ('wood-cut illustrations in the text'). Sometimes, elliptically, the description might simply read 'cuts'.

Since the technique of the wood-cut was already well known before the invention of printing it was natural that the wood-cut should be employed in the very first printed books when there was a call for illustration. As well as being used for illustration, the wood-cut technique was used to produce printer's devices, ornamental borders to pages, vignettes and **initials**, that is, decorative initial letters at the beginning of a chapter or paragraph.

By the end of the eighteenth century the wood-cut technique had come to be despised by many printers. It leant itself to quick and easy exploitation and had become identified with popular, mass-market books. It took the efforts of Thomas Bewick (1753-1825) to restore the technique to some artistic standing. Bewick invented, or reinvented, the technique of working across the end-grain of the wood rather than along the grain, as with the conventional wood-cut. The wood most commonly used by Bewick was from the box tree. Box is a particularly hard wood, with a very compact grain which permits a much more delicate engraving. Wood-cuts produced by this technique are almost always small-scale, a consequence of the fact that the engraver is using a cross-section of the wood. Sometimes three or four cross-sections would be fastened together to provide a larger working surface. Bewick produced a number of books in the 1790's and 1800's depicting British wildlife. These books are for the most part octavo in format, with the illustrations in the text, and often with attractive head- and tail-pieces.

The technique of working across the end-grain is sometimes described as 'wood engraving', to distinguish it from the ordinary wood-cut. (While the wood cut is *cut* with a knife, the wood engraving is *engraved* by means of a graver.) Frequently, however, the terms are used indiscriminately, not least by booksellers.

In the third quarter of the nineteenth century the coloured wood engraving enjoyed a brief vogue as a cheaper rival to chromolithography, which is discussed later. Again, perhaps because of the general prejudice against wood-block, the coloured wood engraving tended to be confined to popular - and cheap - annuals and magazines. In the later nineteenth century its most noted exponent, largely in the field of children's books, was Edmund Evans.

The art of the wood engraver has undergone something of a renaissance in the twentieth century, particularly in Britain, where, since the 1930's, large numbers of books have been produced with illustrations by artists such as Claire Leighton, C.F. Tunnicliffe, John Nash, Gwen Raverat, Robert Gibbings, and Blair Hughes-Stanton. Many of these works are on aspects of natural history or the countryside. They are often very attractive, 'collectable' - and still relatively cheap!

Intaglio Printing

Intaglio printing is printing from the incised parts of a material which has been cut. The commonest type of material used in this form of printing is metal, commonly either copper or steel. The metal takes the form of a **plate** - a flat, smooth sheet - rather than a block. By extension, 'plate' also refers to the finished illustration. A book may be described as having 'numerous plates' or, less fortunately, as 'lacking two plates'. **Copper plate** and **steel plate** are expressions often used by booksellers to describe the type of illustration in a book, though without being specific as to the method of engraving. A **plate book** is a book valuable solely or largely for its plates.

The **plate mark** is the line indented around the margins of the paper and is an incidental result of the printing process. With intaglio printing it is the parts of the plate that have been cut away that hold the ink and which will print. Once the design has been cut the plate is covered with ink and then wiped clean, leaving ink standing only in the incisions. When the plate is placed in the press, great pressure has to be applied to the paper since it is being forced slightly into the incisions to take up the ink. The plate mark results from this pressure, marking as it does the edge of the metal plate. The presence of a plate mark is an almost certain indicator that the illustration is of an intaglio type. (The one main exception concerns modern facsimile reproductions, where the printer is not above impressing a false plate mark around the image to convey an air of age.) The absence of a plate mark, however, does not indicate that the illustration is not of the intaglio type. The paper may have been trimmed in the binding; or with steel plates in particular several illustrations may have been engraved on a single plate, with a single sheet being printed which then has to be cut.

The nature of the printing process involved with intaglio illustration explains why the illustration cannot be printed simultaneously with a piece of text from ordinary type. Any attempt to do so would entail such pressure being brought upon the type that it would probably break. There is also the fact that the paper used for intaglio printing is substantially thicker than that used for ordinary printing from type. This difference is very noticeable to sight and touch when the two are set side by side. So intaglio illustrations are always 'separate' from the text, in the sense that they are printed separately, using a different technique, and bound in, or glued into the book during the binding. And when a book with such illustrations is collated, the illustrations will always be considered separately.

When discussing relief printing I said that illustrations 'in the text' are almost always wood-cut. An exception should be mentioned here, namely, where an intaglio engraving has been printed on a sheet, which has then been put through the press a second time to produce the printed matter. With this type of illustration, which isn't very common, the plate mark will be evidence of the intaglio process. Moreoever, when booksellers are describing such an illustration they will generally avoid the expression 'in the text' and specify the technique employed.

YORK,
From Severus's Hills.

Drawn by Cha.s Cope. Engraved by John Cousen

KIRKSTALL ABBEY N.E

Published by Longman & Co. London and Robinson & Hernaman, Leeds. January 1st 1827.

Typical copper engraving of the late eighteenth century (top) and typical steel engraving of the early nineteenth century.

Of the two metals employed for the plate, copper has been in use since the very earliest times, with artists and engravers producing copper plate illustration since the fifteenth century. Copper continued in use until the early years of the nineteenth century. The steel plate was introduced about the 1820's but had a relatively short life, being replaced by various forms of photo-mechanical reproduction by about the 1870's. Dating can be a useful tool when attempting to distinguish different types of illustration one from another. For example, if the illustration was printed before about 1820 it is very unlikely to be from a steel plate.

Two more features of metal engraving may be mentioned while on the subject of comparing and distinguishing. Firstly, copper is a much softer metal than steel, therefore the lines that are cut into the metal need to be that much further apart if the intervening metal is not be crushed in the press thereby destroying the engraving. Steel being a very hard metal, the lines can be cut extremely close together without running the same risk. It follows that the finished effect of a copper plate illustration is often slightly less refined, or sophisticated, than that of a steel engraving. This is not a comment on the relative skills of the artist or engraver but simply on the constraints imposed by the materials.

The second distinguishing feature concerns the colour of the finished print. Copper engravings tend very often, if not normally, to have a brownish-grey appearance, rather than the solid black of a steel engraving.

The simplest form of intaglio engraving is the **line engraving**, with the engraver cutting, or more accurately, scratching a series of lines in the plate with one or more of a series of special tools. The resulting illustration resembles a line drawing.

A variation of the line engraving introduces the idea of tone. Tone - light and dark, mass, - can be achieved through a variety of means, possibly the simplest of which is the **dry-point**. In dry-point engraving, the engraver does not remove the burr thrown up by the action of cutting into the plate. When the plate is inked this burr holds some of the ink and the plate prints with a soft, hazy line instead of the sharp, clean line of the simple line engraving. Copper, being the softer metal, lends itself much more readily to the dry-point technique. The drawback is that the burr soon wears away under the pressure of the press and thus print runs are necessarily short. This drawback can be overcome by the use of steel plates, or copper plates faced with steel.

Another technique for introducing tone into the illustration is by the use of **stipple**. Stippling consists in running a special tool over the surface of the plate to produce a series of small indentations. When inked and printed the effect is of small dots packed more or less closely together, according to the number of times the tool has been run over the plate. Stipple can be very basic, with each individual dot clearly visible; it can be very sophisticated, with subtle gradations from dark to light. Stipple is often used in conjunction with line engraving.

The **mezzotint** is preeminently a tonal form of engraving. In this technique the entire plate is first worked over with a curved, serrated tool called a rocker, which has the effect of throwing up burr in all directions. As with dry-point, it is the burr that holds the ink. If the plate is inked and printed at this stage it will print a uniform black. The engraver works from black to white, using tools such as scrapers and burnishers to remove more or less of the burr depending on the degree of light and dark required. If the burr is removed in its entirety from part of the plate, that part will 'print' white. The mezzotint technique found favour with, among others, John Constable, who deemed it worthy enough to be used to produce engravings of some his paintings, with David Lucas the engraver. As with dry-point the plate must either be of steel or be steel-faced if long print runs are required, though the best effects are achieved with copper.

It might be argued that both dry-point and mezzotint are not pure forms of intaglio engraving since the printing in both cases is done at least in part from the surface of the plate, if not from a raised surface (the burr which stands proud of the surface). For all practical purposes this point is of academic interest only. The printing process is similar in all cases of intaglio engraving, the only likely difference being variations in the amount of pressure applied in the press.

(The term 'mezzotint' has occasionally been used of late to describe what is in fact a variation of stipple engraving. The plate is treated with the rocker to produce a dense mass of holes which, without further work, would print black. The engraver then removes these holes by polishing and scraping to produce the portions of the plate that will not take the ink, ie., that will 'print' white. The difference is that the ink is held by the holes cut into the plate, whereas with true mezzotint the ink is held by the burr thrown up by the rocker.)

Etching is another form of intaglio printing, though instead of the plate being cut with a tool it is eaten into, or 'bitten', by acid. The plate is covered with a resinous wax, or 'ground', which is acid resistant. The design is drawn on the plate, removing the wax in the process to expose the metal beneath. The plate is then dipped in a bath of acid and the acid eats into the metal that has been exposed. The plate is removed from the bath, wiped clean of wax, then inked and printed in the normal way. Although strictly a line process, tone can be created by removing the plate from the acid bath after a short interval, 'stopping' various parts of the plate - that is, re-covering parts of the cut area with wax - and reinserting the plate in the acid. The parts that remain unstopped will receive a second bite of the acid, and those parts of the plate, when printed, will hold more ink and therefore print darker. The basic principle of etching is extremely simple. However, great variations can be achieved depending simply on the materials used: copper, magnesium or zinc plates; different kinds of ground; different strengths and types of acid.

The great advantage of etching over other forms of intaglio engraving is that it permits a much more free-hand style of illustration. Instead of cutting metal with a tool, the engraver is simply drawing in wax, as though using a pencil or crayon. This is why many etchings are executed by the artist personally and not interpreted by a professional engraver. During the seventeenth century, the great age of the etching, many of the foremost artists of the day produced etchings, though not usually for book illustration.

Soft-ground etching is a variation of the etching technique. The plate is first covered with a granulated ground and a piece of slightly adhesive paper is then laid over it. The design is drawn on the paper. The action of the pencil on the paper makes some of the ground adhere to the underside of the paper when it is lifted off. However, the ground is not lifted off in a clean line. The plate is then treated with acid, as an ordinary etching. The resulting print gives a rather flaky effect, similar to the appearance of crayon over rough paper.

Aquatint is another form of intaglio engraving which employs acid as the active medium. In this process, acid-resistant powdered resin in granular form is dusted over the plate and the plate then gently heated. The action of the acid serves to melt the granules sufficiently for them to adhere to the plate, which is then treated in the acid bath. Great varieties of tone can be achieved by varying the quality of the powdered resin - coarse or fine - as well as the amounts laid over different parts of the plate.

An example of an etching c.1880's

Hand-coloured aquatint from a book of travels, 1819.

Aquatint was invented by a Frenchman in the 1760's and was quickly adopted by many publishers of the more expensive illustrated book. However, it is important to realise that, as far as book illustration is concerned, the aquatint was generally finished with hand-colouring. With many of the more sumptuous books it is in practice often hard to discern the printed foundation to the hand-colouring. The finished effect is very like that of an original water-colour, from which is derived the name of the process, 'aqua-tint'.

The great age of the aquatint was from about the 1770's to the 1820's. Rudolf Ackermann was possibly the most influential publisher using the technique in this period. A typical work of his is *The Microcosm of London*, a quarto work in three volumes issued between 1808 and 1810, containing around 100 plates of London views, all finely hand-coloured. He published similar works on the Universities of Oxford and Cambridge, on public schools and on abbeys and cathedrals. The cost of hand-colouring each plate ensured that these were all expensive productions, even at the time of publication. Nowadays, these works fetch many thousands of pounds apiece at auction.

A more modest worker in the same field was William Gilpin, an antiquarian and traveller who visited many parts of the British Isles from the 1780's to the 1800's. *Observations on the River Wye* (1789) and *Observations on the Coasts of Hampshire, Sussex and Kent* (1804) are two typical titles of his. Many of his works are illustrated with aquatint engravings though, unusually, these aquatints were not hand-coloured.

The most important reference work in the field of hand- coloured plate books is probably by R.V. Tooley. *English Books with Coloured Plates 1790 to 1860. A Bibliographical Account of the most Important Books illustrated by English Artists in Colour Aquatint and Colour Lithography* was first published in 1954. It has recently been reprinted and copies on the secondhand market are easy to find and cheap to buy.

Planographic Printing

Planographic printing is printing from the surface of a block or plate, unlike relief and intaglio, which both involve cutting into the surface. One of the most important forms of planographic printing as far as book illustration is concerned is the **lithograph**.

The lithographic process is based on the mutual attraction and repulsion of water and grease. The block originally used in lithography was a stone ('litho' is Greek for 'stone'), the surface of which is polished flat and smooth. The design is drawn on the surface of the stone with a special lithographic pencil or crayon. The particular peculiarity of this instrument is that it contains a high proportion of grease. Once the design has been drawn, the surface of the stone is dampened. The slightly porous quality of the stone results in the water being retained on the surface of the block except where the crayon has been applied, the greasy quality of the crayon ensuring that the water is repelled. The surface of the block is then inked over, and now the process of attraction and repulsion works in reverse. The ink used in lithography is of a particularly greasy kind, so the parts of the block which are damp - ie., those parts of the block which do not carry the design - reject the ink, while those parts which do carry the design attract the ink. The block is now ready for printing.

The lithographic process was invented in Germany in the 1790's but only came into general use in England in the 1820's. As with aquatint, which it rapidly replaced, it was seized on by publishers and printers and exploited in a large number of illustrated works. However, as with aquatint, the majority of lithographic plates were still hand-coloured after printing. Uncoloured lithographic illustration was perhaps more popular on the Continent than in England. One of the greatest exponents of the art in the middle of the century was the French artist Honoré Daumier, who used it to great effect in his caricatures.

The hey-day of the hand-coloured lithograph was from the 1820's to the 1860's and saw the publication of a great variety of illustrated books reflecting the cultural pursuits and interests of early Victorian Britain - topographical view books, antiquities, botanical and horticultural subjects, field sports and the armed services. Books of foreign views were also popular, especially books reflecting life in the British Empire.

John James Audubon is perhaps the most famous name in hand-coloured lithographic illustration, with his extraordinary *Birds of America* published between 1827 and 1838, in elephant folio format and containing over 400 illustrations.

Colour was added to the lithographic process in the 1850's. **Chromolithographs**, or 'chromos' for short, constitute the first commercially successful attempt at printing in colour. In early chromlithography one colour only was printed at a time, thus the design on the stone had to be

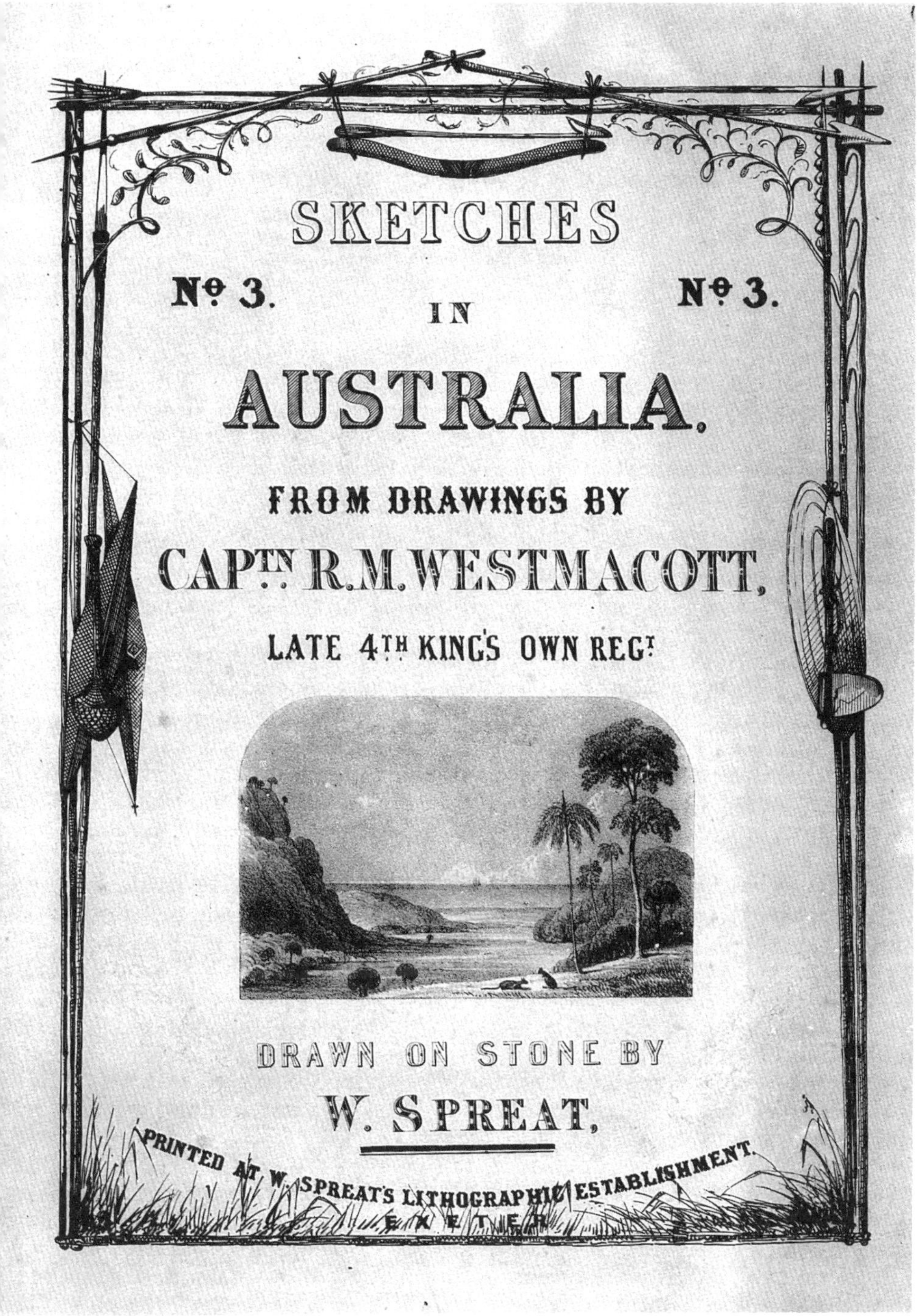

Typical title-page from a book of lithographic views, mid-nineteenth century.

reworked for each separate colour and the sheet put through the press any number of times, corresponding to the number of colours employed. A crucial aspect of this sort of colour printing is **register**, that is, the alignment of the colours against one another so that they neither overlap nor show a gap between. The complexities involved can easily be imagined when one realises that some chromos employ ten or more colours.

Owen Jones was one of the earliest, and most accomplished chromolithographers. His *Grammar of Ornament* - a guide to style and decor for designers, architects and draughtsmen - was published in 1856 and reprinted many times right into the twentieth century.

For a brief while, the chromolithographic process enjoyed an enormous vogue in mid-Victorian England, with publishers almost vying with each other to exploit the technique in every conceivable way - not just for illustration but for ornament and decoration as well. Large numbers of books were produced solely with a view to taking advantage of the technique. Given the prevailing view of Victorian England as conventional, if not dull and staid, the rampant luxuriance of many of these productions may come as a surprise - reds, yellows, violets, blues, greens, oranges, silver and gold all bursting from the page. If anything, the chromolithographic technique was used significantly more for decoration and ornament than for illustration proper, and this is one pointer to distinguishing the chromolithograph from other types of colour illustration. Another distinguishing feature is that the colours of a chromolithograph possess a noticeably 'flat' quality in contrast with, for example, hand-colouring. This is a feature which the eye can soon come to recognise with a little training.

By the middle of the nineteenth century we begin finally to see the development of what might be called modern methods of reproduction. The use of photography and photo-chemical processes was being explored in the 1850's with a technique called wet-collodion; the half-tone process was being developed not much later, along with photogravure. The principle of lithography showed itself amenable to adaptation and improvement in a number of ways, not least in offset lithography, a process in which the image is not printed directly onto the paper but onto a rubber roller which then transfers the image to the paper. Much jobbing printing is still produced by offset litho.

Apart from those with a specialist interest in the subject, a knowledge of the technicalities of these processes is of small interest or use to collectors and dealers.

Finally, I should mention books illustrated with real photographs. Almost from the beginnings of photography publishers realised the possibilities of the new invention, and books illustrated with **mounted photographs** - that is, original photographs glued to blank leaves - now constitute a significant collecting field.

Breakers and Breaking

A **breaker** is a book that is of interest and value solely or primarily for the plates. The book will be *broken*, the plates removed and sold individually. 'Breaker' may also mean a copy of a book which, though it would not ordinarily be treated in this way, is in such poor condition that it is fit for nothing else. 'Breaker' also refers to the person who does the breaking.

The subject of breaking often arouses much passion both inside and outside the trade. There are those who argue that it is somehow immoral to destroy a book in this way, indeed, in *any* way. (This sense of outrage may in part be explained by a fetishistic attitude towards the book. The book whatever its particular subject matter, represents culture, intellectual progress, artistic endeavour, and as such should be treated with respect, venerated even, *qua* physical object. There are those who cannot bear to throw a book away. Many a time have I had to perform this melancholy task on behalf of customers who have offered for sale unsaleable books.)

The typical breaker is an early- to mid-nineteenth century quarto book of steel-engraved topographical views. Such books were produced in their thousands, taking advantage of the superior qualities of steel as an engraving medium and to satisfy the burgeoning demand among the middle classes for some knowledge, however superficial, of the country in which they lived. They are the equivalent of today's photographic essay on aspects of the British countryside. Typical titles are Allom and Rose, *The British Switzerland; or Picturesque Rambles in the English Lakes* (1858) with 76 plates; Barber, *Picturesque Illustrations of the Isle of Wight* (1835), 41 plates; Bartlett, *The Scenery and Antiquities of Ireland* (1846), 2 volumes with 120 plates; Beattie, *Scotland Illustrated in a Series of Views* (1838), 2 volumes with 119 plates; Ingram, *Memorials of Oxford* (1837),

3 volumes with 100 plates. A useful reference work for this kind of book is Mervyn Holloway's *Steel Engravings in Nineteenth Century Topographical Books* (1977).

It is a fair guess that the people who bought such books spent more time looking at the pictures than they did reading the text, much as people do today. It may be argued that nothing is lost to society or culture by breaking such books as these, even that more pleasure is afforded to more people by the individual plates being mounted and put on a wall. Kept in the book they tend to remain unviewed, like photographs in the family album.

It is important to remember that the colouring on steel plates is almost certainly modern and not 'contemporary', ie., executed at the time of issue.

The simplest way of assessing the value of a run-of-the-mill topographical breaker is on the basis of so much per plate - a pound or two or three. However, this procedure is fairly crude; some plates are more interesting than others. Generally speaking, interior views are of little or no value; views of obscure country houses can have some modest value but only if the building is still extant; churches, cathedrals and abbeys are of little interest apart from the very obvious ones (Bath Abbey, York Minster &c) in towns with a strong tourist trade; the value of scenic views can vary considerably depending on how interesting the view actually is, what it contains and the part of the country concerned. Best of all are views of towns, even if utterly unrecognisable today, street scenes, thoroughfares and famous buildings. Sea-scapes are also a very popular theme. So a print-seller looking at a potential topographical breaker will be concerned to decide just what proportion of the plates he or she can actually use rather than simply totalling the quantity and working out a price from that. Another very important consideration is the title of the plate. In most cases the plate will carry underneath the illustration a title or name, identifying the scene. If there is no identifying title - if the illustration, for example, is identified on the page of facing text - then the value of the plate is considerably reduced. The potential buyer needs to be told what it is he or she is looking at - Guildford in the 1820's bears scant resemblance to the same town in the 1990's.

Fashion is also important in the breaking trade, both as concerns British views and foreign views. Scotland (no disrespect to the Scots) is more or less 'out' at the moment, probably because the market, never very large, is now saturated. North Wales is more sought after than South Wales. In the case of foreign topography France and the Low Countries have not been of much importance for a long while now. Views in Germany and Switzerland, by contrast, are very much in demand.

At the other end of the breaking scale are those books, more or less serious and scholarly, which contain only a handful of plates as an adjunct to the text. Such books are not breakers in the strict sense of the term, though this does not inhibit people from removing one or two of the more attractive and interesting plates. A book of this sort that has lost a plate or two is generally a sorry affair and a burden to the bookseller who acquires it. He will probably only be able to sell it for a small fraction of the price a complete copy would fetch.

Topographical books, whether with steel or copper plates, aquatints or lithographs, are the most obvious candidates for breaking. Another significant field is natural history, in particular plates of flowers and birds with contemporary hand-colouring. If the steel-engraved plate represents the cheap and cheerful end of the market, natural history plates, hand-coloured aquatints and lithographs, represent the expensive end, with books selling for the equivalent of several hundred pounds per plate. Audubon's *Birds of America* has already been mentioned. Another typical breaker of the same calibre is Thornton's *Temple of Flora* (1812).

Illustrated newspapers of the nineteenth century are also popular with breakers, especially *The Illustrated London News*. The desirable illustrations are those from wood-blocks and again, if coloured, the colouring is modern.

Nowadays, almost anything is grist to the breaker's mill - books illustrated by the likes of Arthur Rackham, Edmund Dulac and Kate Greenaway; books with colour reproductions of topographical water-colours such as the series produced by publishers A. & C. Black in the 1920's and 1930's; magazines of the 1920's to 1950's for their advertisments with a 'period' flavour; old gazeteers for their town plans. Whatever the ethics of breaking - if there is such a thing - the practice is well-entrenched and a significant part of the antiquarian and secondhand book trade. It has played an important role in driving up prices in the last twenty to thirty years. It has even, in some instances, created a market where none existed before.

Available from the PBFA byMail Order

Folding Bookshelves

As used at book fairs. In natural beech with three shelves. Each unit measures 37" x 27" with shelf depth of 11". Light, freestanding and stackable. Please phone for price and delivery charge.

Directory of Members

Lists over 650 antiquarian and secondhand booksellers by name, county and speciality. Also includes sections on catalogue booksellers and those who offer valuations plus a section on suppliers of book-related services. £2.50 incl. postage & packing

Calendar of PBFA Book Fairs

A pocket guide to all PBFA book fairs for the current year. Free on request.

Chilhood Recollected: EARLY CHILDREN'S BOOKS FROM THE LIBRARY OF MARJORIE MOON.

By Brian Alderson & Marjorie Moon.Published by PBFA. A catalogue produced to accompany the Marjorie Moon Exhibition at Oxford, September 1994. Full bibliographical descriptions of the 138 exhibits plus notes. 2 appendices on the publishing history of *Little Jack Horner* and *Holiday House*. A must for the children's book collector. £12.95 plus 80p postage.

<u>Terms and conditions of sale</u>

Cash with order please. Credit card customers may order and pay by telephone.

All items are normally despatched on the same day but please allow 28 days for delivery

PBFA: The Old Coach House, 16 Melbourn Street,
Royston, Hertfordshire, SG8 7BZ.

Tel: 01763 248400; Fax 01763 248921

MasterCard P.B.F.A. VISA

Condition, Conservation and Repair

The subjects of condition and conservation are so closely related that they are best treated together. Discussion of the condition of a particular copy of a book will, if the condition is anything less than perfect, entail a discussion of the value of that copy relative to the value of a copy in fine condition; if the condition is far from perfect, and if the book is potentially valuable, there will also be discussion of the merits of conservation work. What I am concerned with in this chapter are the general principles involved in the conservation and repair of books rather than any particular techniques, a subject which is more for the book binder and paper restorer.

It would be difficult to exaggerate the importance attached to condition by both collectors and booksellers. Condition is one of the main determinants of value. A copy of a book in very good condition can fetch many times the amount realised by a copy in merely 'good' condition, or worse. Copies in 'fair' or poor condition may often have little or no value. If a bookseller catalogues a 'very good' copy of a book at, say, £50 it would not be surprising if he or she refused to catalogue a less than good copy at any price at all. A price of £50 suggests that the book is not uncommon; potential buyers may be reasonably sure of finding sooner rather than later a copy in good condition at or about that price. So it would not be worth the bookseller's while to bother with cheaper, poorer copies. This is not to say that there is not a market for copies in poor condition, rather that the market is a 'grey' market. The interested reader may pick up such a copy by chance in a secondhand bookshop, but few booksellers, whether operating by catalogue or through a shop, will go out of their way to stock a poor copy. A fair or poor copy may have come their way inadvertently, as the result of the purchase of a job lot. Rather than throw the book away, the bookseller might put it on the shelf at a more or less token price. But if someone walks in off the street and offers to sell him a fair or poor copy he is unlikely to want to buy it.

Some of the terms in general use to describe the overall condition of the book have already been mentioned. A complete list, in descending order is: **mint** (as new); **fine** (nearly mint); **very good** (showing some signs of wear, but acceptable in relation to the age of the book); **good** (that is to say, *merely* good); **fair** and **poor**. (While these descriptions might have an air of objectivity about them, their application is in the end subjective; one bookseller's 'very good' copy may be another bookseller's 'good' copy.)

A **reading copy** is a copy fit only for the purpose for which it was originally intended, that is, to be read. The text is complete but that is all that can be said in the book's favour. **Working copy** means much the same as 'reading copy' but tends to be used with books of a more technical or practical nature. A book that is **distressed** is not a book in need of tranquillisers but one that life has certainly treated harshly, the effects of which treatment the bookseller may or may not describe in his catalogue. **Ex-library** (**ex-lib**) denotes a copy removed from a library. The value of the copy will depend crucially on how many library markings there are on the book - stamps, bookplates, ticket pockets, pencil and ink marks. There are other, more specific terms in use too numerous to mention. A glance at any bookseller's catalogue will reveal books that are thumbed, spotted, foxed, worn, faded, annotated and so on. Alternatively, a copy might be bright, fresh, clean, or simply 'nice'. And catalogues in general are a useful guide to current terminology, always allowing for individual interpretation and idiosyncracy.

Some cataloguers are given to euphemism (they are, after all, trying to sell their books, and often have to make the best of a bad job). The covers of the book may be described as 'sunned', an adjective which conjurs up for me at least an image of the book taking its ease in the garden on a summer's day. What is *meant* is 'faded'. Other cataloguers face the facts squarely, if not grimly, describing, for example, the binding of the book, somewhat alarmingly, as 'shot', meaning decrepit or ruined. Then there are the professional optimists, the booksellers who list in detail a series of hideous defects only to conclude their description with the phrase 'very good'.

Books that are offered for sale **as seen** or **with all faults** (**w.a.f.**) should be treated with caution. The book is likely to be defective in some way, or at least in very bad condition. The vendor almost certainly has not collated the book, and generally offers it for sale not subject to return.

Given that books were originally intended to be *used* it is unsurprising that they should show signs of use over time. The degree of wear acceptable to collectors is to some extent determined by the age of the book and the particular collecting field. The first edition of a novel by Trollope may show signs of wear on the covers and yet still be an acceptable copy. The same degree of wear on the covers of a first edition of a Len Deighton novel would not be acceptable since, in theory at least, a copy in pristine condition should not be too difficult to find. (It has to be said that collectors of modern firsts are by far the most fanatical on the question of condition, possibly because there is so little else to distinguish one copy from another.) It would be an over-simplification to state that copies in poor condition never have any value; the greater the value of a copy in good condition or better, the more likely it is that a poor copy will have some modest value. If a fine copy of that Trollope novel were worth £300 to £400, a less than fine copy might range down to £100 or less depending on the amount of wear. On the other hand, an early Grahame Greene novel might be worth £100 to £200 in fine condition and a matter of a few pounds only in merely 'good' condition. (An extreme example noted recently was a copy of Bruce Chatwin's *In Patagonia* (1977) offered for sale in fine condition for £350. The next entry in the catalogue was another copy, also a first edition and in dust wrapper, but an ex-library copy in poor condition. The asking price was £30.)

With truly antiquarian books the position is more complicated, when 'poor condition' might actually mean defective. The same principles apply: how serious is the defect, and how valuable would a copy be without the defect. Sixteenth century bibles lacking a number of leaves at either end are not at all uncommon and can still have some value. The point here is that copies whole and complete are very scarce, so the near impossibility of finding a copy in very good condition, regardless of price, makes the less than good copy acceptable. Put bluntly, the choice is sometimes between a poor copy or no copy at all. (Such books may also be bought with a view to *making up* a copy, that is, making good a deficiency in a second copy by adding leaves from the first, to produce a **made-up copy**.)

Foxing is the most common type of defect affecting the paper on which the book is printed. It consists of brown spots discolouring the paper and is the result of a chemical change within the paper itself. It can be removed by a variety of techniques but the effort is seldom worthwhile. A copy that is 'lightly foxed' would generally be acceptable to most people, always provided there were no other defects. However, many collectors would think twice before committing themselves to the purchase of a copy that was 'heavily foxed'.

Many books suffer at some point in their lives from damp. A degree of damp-staining or water-staining (the two terms are generally interchangeable) is often unavoidable. Whether it is acceptable or not in a given copy is in the end a matter of taste, as with foxing. Again as with foxing, damp marks can often be removed with some trouble and expense, though the operation usually involves taking the book apart completely. Almost the only case where foxing and water-staining are not drawbacks is with books that are going to be broken up for their plates. The individual plates can be cleaned quite easily, and since the book is not going to be put back together again little expense is involved.

The process of cleaning the pages of a book is known as **washing**. This might be necessary not only to remove foxing and damp-staining but also general dirt, the result simply of long use rather than neglect. The book would probably need to be removed from its binding, the stitching undone and each leaf cleaned separately. On completion the book would be resewn and rebound. Books that have been washed generally betray the fact by an unnatural whiteness of the paper with a corresponding slight greying of the ink.

The third common disfigurement of paper is **off-setting**, that is, the tranference of ink from an engraved illustration to the facing printed page. This occurs most commonly in older books, of the eighteenth century in particular, usually where the engraving is from a copper plate. The book has been left closed for decades at a time and during that time part of the ink of the engraving has stained the facing page, leaving a mirror image of the original illustration, generally in more or less dark brown. Some books were bound with **tissue guards** (often abbreviated to **guards**) bound between the engraving and the facing page to prevent off-setting.

Worming results from the activities of maggots and other grubs eating their way through the paper and leaving a variety of holes. As long as there is no loss of text (see below) a copy that is wormed may probably still be acceptable.

Tears to a leaf constitute another problem for the collector. In many types of book a tear of any sort is sufficient to render the book valueless. The more 'antiquarian' the book, the more likely it is that a tear will be tolerated, but only if the tear is clean and does not involve any loss of text. To make plain the position, booksellers will use such phrases in their catalogues as 'torn without loss', meaning 'no loss of printed matter'. If the leaf is 'torn with loss', no matter how slight the loss of printed matter, the copy is probably best avoided. Many booksellers will refuse to handle any book that has such a defect. However, as with everything, there are exceptions. The example of the early Bible already cited is one such. If the book is exceptionally rare and desirable then a copy with a torn leaf, or a leaf or leaves lacking, may be acceptable, though its value will always be substantially less than that of a whole copy. In some cases, the bookseller will go to the trouble of having a facsimile made of the missing leaf and binding it in.

Repairs to a damaged title-leaf or other leaf with text on the recto only might involve **mounting**, that is, backing the leaf onto another piece of paper and then either resewing the leaf into the book or simply gluing it into place. Worn margins of a leaf might be similarly treated while still in situ. A leaf with printing on both recto and verso might, if damaged, be mounted on a special transparent paper.

Apart from missing leaves in the body of the text, probably the most common defect of the book (as opposed to the binding) is a missing leaf. Missing blank leaves at either end are an irritant but usually not fatal to value; the older the book, the slighter the wound. With nineteenth-century books in publisher's cloth, the absence of a blank leaf is generally more serious, since copies with the blank are more easily available. The same applies to the half-title, though since the half-title actually bears some printed matter the problem is that more serious. A copy of our notional nineteenth-century novel without the half- title with which it was issued will often be significantly less valuable than a copy which still displays it.

A factor also to consider is how, or when, the blank or half-title went missing. Was it removed at the time of first binding? (perhaps bearable); was it removed during a later rebinding? (worse); has it been torn out of the book by a previous owner? (very bad).

As was noted when discussing breakers, plates or other pictorial matter are frequently lacking, almost always torn out or cut out of the book. (If the missing plate was not bound into the book in the first place, the matter is slightly less serious, but only slightly. A situation that occasionally occurs is for an engraved illustration to be noted in the list of illustrations without ever having been printed. The publisher intended to produce the plate but for some reason did not manage it. So the book without the plate can be described as complete.) If there is a list of illustrations, then collation is quite easy, though it should be born in mind that the binder very often did not bind the plates in the order or in the places laid down in the list of illustrations. It was also common practice to take one illustration and place it as a frontispiece, without any indication of this in the list of illustrations. If there is no list of illustrations whereby to check for completeness and if no bibliography is to hand which might say how many illustrations there ought to be, then one way of proceeding is to examine the inner margins of all the leaves for evidence of anything having been removed. It is virtually impossible to remove anything such as a plate without leaving some sort of trace. A useful quick check involves holding the closed book firmly between two hands and examining either the top or bottom edge close to the spine. If a plate has been cut out of the book the stub left behind is usually quite visible.

Collating the book, by signature, page or leaf, will reveal any missing leaves, though because of the vagaries of printing practice collation of the peliminary leaves may be more difficult. If the book was originally issued with advertisments then they too should ideally be present though their lack would not constitute a defect in the strict sense since they are not part of the book. (I say 'in the strict sense' since collectors can become obsessed with the presence or absence of advertisments. As already mentioned, many of Charles Dickens' works were originally issued in part form. These parts were bound in printed wrappers, and included with each part were a variety of advertisments - for patent medicines, hair oil, dress clothes and the like. The presence or absence of some or all of these advertisments can make a substantial difference to the value of Dickens' novels 'in the parts'. To further complicate matters, some parts were quickly reprinted due to special demand, and sometimes reprinted with different advertisments. A bibliographer's nightmare!)

The free endpapers of a book are frequently found to be missing. A common explantion for the loss of the front free endpaper is that it bore some offensive, incriminating or otherwise objectionable matter (an owner's name, a book plate, a library stamp) and has been removed by a subsequent owner. I once bought a box of books from a customer in my shop. When he had pocketed the money he proceeded to take each book and tear out the endpaper, which bore his name. When I objected, he informed me that he did not wish to have books bearing his name circulating in the secondhand market. I had to point out to him that while his name in the books would add nothing to their value (see 'Signatures, Inscriptions and Annotations'), the loss of the endpapers would certainly detract from that value. Since the endpaper is technically part of the binding rather than the book itself, its loss may be considered rather less serious than the loss of anything else. They can in many instances be replaced fairly easily.

When repair or conservation are being considered, the question of **original state** has to be taken into account. We have already met this expression in several different contexts. Briefly, 'original state' means that state in which the book was originally offered for sale. Original state is highly prized and almost always to be valued over any other state. The difficulty with repair and conservation is that, necessary though they may be, they necessarily detract from that original state. A balance has always to be struck between preserving what was originally present and conserving, in the sense of treating, what was originally present in order to prevent it from deteriorating altogether.

In practice, questions of original state arise most frequently with reference to the binding of the book, in particular publishers' cloth bindings. It is almost always better to preserve the original cloth binding than to have it replaced by anything else, even the most elaborate and expensive calf. A competent binder can remove the cloth case from the book, clean it, repair any minor defects and put it back on the book. Such a book has been, in the jargon, **recased**. Even such a copy would be worth less, all things being equal, than a copy in good condition which had not been thus treated. But it would probably be worth more than a copy whose original case had been discarded.

With leather bindings before the introduction of cloth in the 1820's, the same principle applies: better to preserve if at all possible the contemporary binding, whatever that may be, than to replace it. If the spine of the book has disintegrated but the boards are still in reasonable condition it is preferable to retain the boards and replace the spine. With seventeenth- or eighteenth-century books in original boards it is, again, preferable to retain the boards rather than rebind the book.

The question of repair most often occurs with reference to the binding of the book. 'Is it worth rebinding?' booksellers are often asked. The answer depends on what is meant by 'worth'. Financial 'worth' must be distinguished from other kinds. If it is a case of a book that has sentimental value, a book that has been in the family for years, a book that has a particular appeal to a particular person, it may well be 'worth' rebinding, that is, spending a more or less modest sum on having the covers either repaired or replaced in order to allow the book to be comfortably read. However, in the majority of cases, the cost of rebinding will not be recouped if the book is offered for sale.

From a commercial point of view rebinding is a very different matter. An example will illustrate the point. A bookseller prices a nice copy of an eighteenth-century work in a good contemporary calf binding at £100. The same book newly rebound in calf he might price at a discount of twenty to thirty percent, £70 to £80. But the cost of binding a standard octavo book in full calf might easily reach £50 to £60. From these figures alone it should be obvious that for the dealer to bear the cost of rebinding and then attempt to sell the book would be economic nonsense. The margin of profit is too small. Moreover, I have allowed nothing for the original purchase price of the book. I have also assumed that the text of the rebound copy is as fresh and clean as that of the copy which doesn't need rebinding, something which is unlikely to be the case.

A not very satisfactory solution would be to have the book bound in half- or quarter-leather. This would reduce the cost of materials and allow a greater margin, though the selling price might be slightly less than that of a copy in full leather. In a more radical approach, the bookseller might abandon any attempt to recreate the old binding and opt for plain cloth, or even half- or quarter-cloth with paper-covered boards. This would bring the binding costs down substantially, but would also probably reduce the selling price. It may also be that the presence of rather utilitarian modern boards will put off a number of potential customers, despite a lower price - the binding is simply not to their taste. One way of avoiding a decision adopted by booksellers selling within the trade is to offer the book in its original 'distressed' state, passing the problem onto the purchaser.

With older books it may be necessary to take into account the historical value of the binding. Does the binding, despite its poor condition, provide information about the book's publication? Does it yield information about contemporary binding practice? With sixteenth-century books, in particular, binders were in the habit of using scraps of old manuscripts and discarded sheets as part of the binding. Nowadays, these scraps are often more interesting and valuable than the book they help to protect.

The following extract is taken from a bibliographer's description, published in 1905, of a particular copy of the first Folio Shakespeare:

'[This copy] will serve as a warning against the folly of having books rebound merely because their bindings are old and shabby. Thirty years ago [ie., in the 1870's] this very copy was taken to a large and first-rate English Library with a view to finding out what might be best done for it. The advice given was that it should be re-bound in full morocco. Fortunately that advice was not followed; had it been, the Shakespeare would have emerged from the binder's hands beautiful perhaps in appearance, but all which could tell of its past history would have perished amid the rubbish and waste of a binder's workshop. Today, it exhibits one of the very few Shakespeare bindings which show no trace whatever of the re-binder's or restorer's hand: the gashes where the iron staple was torn off are still there, with rough edges of broken leather, and the corners still hang limply, as when the injury was first inflicted.'

A possible solution to a problem of this nature, though perhaps not with a book as large as a folio, is to have made a box or slip-case in which the book, in its original binding, can be preserved without the binding suffering further wear.

Every decision to rebind or repair, or to leave well alone, is a judgement arrived at after balancing the various factors outlined above. In some cases the original binding will have deteriorated to such a degree that it simply has to be discarded; in other cases, part or all of the binding may be recoverable. The advice of a professional bookseller or competent binder should be sought before any repairs are undertaken, and it is good policy never to attempt any repairs oneself, unless on a book of absolutely no value. There are few things worse than a book which has been the victim of the amateur repairer.

Bibiliographies

Bibliographies are to the bookseller and collector what maps are to the traveller. Without maps, the traveller may still find his way through the jungle or across the Home Counties, but unless he already knows the area his arrival will be more a matter of luck than judgement. The greater likelihood is that he will spend his time going round in circles. Likewise, a bookseller, faced with a given book, may, without a bibliography, make a guess as to its status, but it remains a guess until a bibliography is consulted to confirm or contradict it.

There are many different types of bibliography, providing different information and serving varying ends: bibliographies of authors, of publishing houses, of topics or themes (angling, the Bible, erotica); of particular libraries, private and public, even of specific books (editions of Isaac Walton's *Compleat Angler*). The specialist bookseller and collector will decide for him or herself which bibliographies are (a) absolutely essential, (b) not quite essential, (c) a useful luxury, or (d) of remote interest. For the general bookseller and the person who collects across a wide range, the rule is that one can never have too many bibliographies. Many booksellers build up a comprehensive collection of bibliographies during their years in business and when they come to retire, if they ever do, the sale of this collection can add handsomely to their pension. For bibliographies almost never go out of fashion; if anything, they tend to hold their real value more than almost any other kind of book.

To discover what bibliographies are available in a given area, the enquirer should consult a bibliography of bibliographies, for example, Theodore Besterman's *A World Bibliography of Bibliographies*, 1947-49 and since revised. This and other guides to reference material should be available at your local library. Some booksellers specialise in bibliography, selling nothing but books about books. Consult one such and you will probably find that he or she knows what bibliographical material has been published in the relevant area.

The author bibliography is probably the most obviously useful. The standard such bibliography will provide, in exhaustive detail, a description of the physical aspects of all the published works of the writer in question. A typical entry will begin with a description of the title-page - what is printed there and how it is laid out; there will follow the book's collation - how many signatures, pages or folios the book consists of and how they are made up; then a description of all the preliminary leaves, with details of what is printed on each of them.

Once the inside of the book has been dealt with, the bibliographer will turn to the outside, to the binding, but normally only if the book was published after the introduction of edition binding by the publisher, almost always in cloth. The colour and texture of the cloth will be described, together with any decoration in gilt or in blind and any labels which may appear on the spine. The bibliographer may then go on to give details of the publication - exact date and number of copies printed. Prefacing the whole entry there may be a brief essay outlining the circumstances of publication.

The point of the author bibliography is to provide the collector and bookseller with a standard of comparison: with the bibliography in one hand and a copy of the book in question in the other, he or she can compare the copy they possess with the description of the ideal or standard copy. If the two copies match perfectly, the bookseller will cite the bibliographical reference after giving the description. It is this rather cryptic note which often appears at the end of the catalogue entry: 'Kirkpatrick A4' (B.J. Kirkpatrick, *A Bibliography of the Works of Katherine Mansfield*; 'Collie IXC' (Michael Collie, *George Gissing: A Bibliography*). (The reader should note that all the names or titles which appear in **bold** in the rest of this chapter are used by booksellers and collectors in a similar way, as abbreviations for the bibliographies in question.)

In many cases, particularly with novelists of the nineteenth century, variations between copies are quite common, especially with regard to the binding. The more comprehensive the bibliography, the more of these variant copies will have been examined and their details noted. Thus the bookseller or collector can check whether the binding on their particular copy is a 'first edition first issue binding', whether it is a 'secondary binding' or merely a 'variant binding' whose status isn't clear.

Many author bibliographies are the product of a collector's enthusiasm. Years spent buying editions of a favourite author, coupled with frustration at the lack of a definitive bibliography, leads them to write one themselves. Most author bibliographies will contain a disclaimer to the effect that the compiler is not prepared to assert that he or she has seen and noted every single edition and variant in existence and will welcome news of any such copy not already noted. It has become a selling point with some booksellers to note an edition or variant that has escaped the compiler of a standard bibliography - **'not in'** Kirkpatrick - with the implication that the book in question must be extremely rare and hence especially valuable.

Another type of bibliography concerns itself with a theme or subject matter rather than the works of a particular writer. An example is A.S. Herbert's *Historical Catalogue of Printed Editions of the English Bible 1521-1961*, commonly abbreviated to **Herbert**. The aim of this bibliography is less to tell us everything there is to know about every edition of the Bible, rather to enable us to identify different editions. This may well entail providing details of signatures and collation but not necessarily. Often it is sufficient to draw attention to a variation in title-pages, or simply to mention the final signature letter. With later Bibles in particular, Herbert generally confines himself to title, imprint and pagination.

A second example of a 'thematic' bibliography is J.H. Woolmer's *Checklist of the Hogarth Press 1917-1938*. (A **checklist** may be described as an abbreviated bibliography, in which the compiler provides less information, often just the author, the title and the date of first publication.) In Woolmer's case, though he styles his work a checklist, the information he provides is in fact quite comprehensive, including pagination and print run.

Other types of bibliography may be described as primary bibliographies in that they deal with large, general collections or libraries. The most important of these is undoubtedly the *British Museum General Catalogue of Printed Books to 1955* with supplementary volumes bringing the catalogue up to date (abbreviated variously to **BMC**, 'British Museum Catalogue' or **BL**, 'British Library'.) The British Library, as it is now generally known, is a copyright library, which means that it should by law receive a copy of every book printed in the U.K. This fact, together with purchases and donations, makes it the most comprehensive holding of printed matter in the country, probably in the world. The information provided in the British Library Catalogue is not as detailed as with an author bibliography, but the sheer comprehensiveness of the holdings means that a listing here is often the only way of tracing a copy of the more obscure items.

On a much smaller scale but a similar principle are the catalogues of the libraries of the University of Oxford (Bodleian Library catalogue) and Edinburgh.

Another example of a primary bibliography is the *Short-Title Catalogue of Books Printed in England, Scotland and Ireland and of English Books Printed Abroad 1475-1640*, originally compiled by A.W. Pollard and G.R. Redgrave. This bibliography is almost universally abbreviated to **S.T.C.**, and an S.T.C. number is near obligatory in catalogues of older books issued by specialist dealers. Again, information is not detailed, among other things, the idea of the 'short title' is to give only sufficient of the title as is necessary to identify the book. The aim of the S.T.C. is to provide a comprehensive listing of all the books that fall within the period so that librarians, booksellers, bibliographers and collectors can know what was actually printed during the time in question, can distinguish different editions from one another, can glean information about publishers as well as authors, and can know where copies of these books are located.

The idea of the short-title catalogue has been taken up since by other bibliographers. Thus there are S.T.C.'s of provincial imprints (books published outside London), while Donald **Wing** extended Pollard and Redgrave to 1700 in his *Short-Title Catalogue of Books Printed in England, Scotland, Ireland, Wales and British America, and of English Books printed in other Countries, 1641-1700.*

The National Union Catalog (**N.U.C.**) details holdings of libraries throughout the U.S.A. The N.U.C. gives details of how many copies have been noted and where they are located. The fact that, for a given entry, only one or two copies are noted is often cited by booksellers as evidence of rarity, and hence value.

The Catalogue Général of the Bibliotheque National in Paris is the French equivalent of the British Library catalogue.

Two primary bibliographies for those with an interest in **incunabula**, that is books printed before 1501, are Ludwig **Hain**, *Repertorium bibliographicum ad annum MD,* published between 1826 and 1838 and since supplemented by various bibliographers, and F.R. **Goff**, *Incunabula in American Libraries,* first isuued in 1919 and since revised.

National bibliographies - as opposed to primary - include W.T. Lowndes *The Bibliographer's Manual of English Literature* published in 1834. This is a much more personal catalogue of books - 'An account of rare, curious and useful books' - in which the compiler has made his own decision as to what is worthy of mention and what not. It is much cited by booksellers as a source of information not easily obtainable elsewhere. The edition most commonly used is that edited and enlarged by H.G. Bohn and issued some thirty years after the original.

Lowndes might be considered the forerunner of *The Cambridge Bibliography of English Literature* (**CBEL**) which provides the most comprehensive guide to works by English authors, listing not only first editions but reprints and revisions as well as works about the author in question. Originally issued in the 1940's, a new edition has recently been completed.

Another example of a national bibliography is **Halkett and Laing**'s *Dictionary of Anonymous and Pseudonymous English Literature* (1882-88). It has been subject to almost continuous revision since that time, not least since unrecorded items are continually coming to light and new information coming to hand in what is by its nature a field of study at once obscure and complicated.

Brunet's *Manuel du Livre et de l'Amateur de Livres* serves something of the same purpose as Lowndes, concentrating on French and Continental literature, while Joseph **Sabin**'s *Bibliotheca Americana. A Dictionary of Books relating to America from its Discovery to the Present Time* is the standard reference work on Americana. The first volume was published in 1868 and the last in 1936.

More specific than these national bibliographies are those which concentrate on just one aspect of the literature of a country such as W.W. **Greg**'s *Bibliography of the English Printed Drama to the Restoration* issued in four volumes between 1939 and 1959, while John **Hayward**'s *English Poetry. A Descriptive Catalogue of First and Early Editions ... from Chaucer to the Present Day* came out in 1947. Michael **Sadleir** published his *XIX Century Fiction. A bibliographical record based on his own collection* in 1951. This has become the standard bibliography on the subject and no specialist bookseller or collector can afford to be without it, not least because it includes material not covered by any author bibliography. Among other things, Sadleir provides much information about the bindings of various editions.

Another type of bibliography deals with books in print, as they were issued or about to be issued. The Company of Stationers was granted a monopoly in printing in the mid-sixteenth century one consequence of which was that every publication had to be licenced. From this there followed a Register of books licenced. The influence of the Stationers's Company, and hence the practice of putting books forward for licensing, declined after the middle of the seventeenth century, but the records of the first hundred years or so of the Register's life provide an interesting insight into contemporary publishing. A transcript of these registers was issued in the late nineteenth century edited by Edward Arber.

A further early example of 'books in print' is the series of publications now known as the **Term catalogues**. These were lists of all the books published in the course of each of the law terms, Hilary, Easter, Trinity and Michaelmas and were issued regularly between 1668 and 1709. They were reprinted early this century in a version edited by Arber. Far more comprehensive and systematic is the *English Catalogue of Books*, which provides the same service for books of the nineteenth and twentieth centuries.

Auction records are another important source of bibliographical information. Both *American Book Prices Current* (ABPC) and the English equivalent, *Book Auction Records* (BAR), have been published throughout this century and not infrequently contain details of books which have escaped all the major bibliographies.

Not strictly a bibliography, but with much useful information is the *Dictionary of National Biography* (**D.N.B.**), sets of which can be found in most public libraries. Also useful for the book collector and bibliographer is the Eleventh edition of the Encyclopedia Britannica. This contains much useful information of a more or less 'antiquarian' nature which was cut from succeeding editions, including biographies of some of the more obscure writers and summary bibliographies of their works.

This is merely an introduction to what is a very large subject; some of the main types of bibliography have been discussed and examples given. The interested collector will search out the bibliographical material most appropriate for his or her purposes and each bibliography consulted will almost certainly lead on to others in a never-ending chain. Booksellers themselves have already been mentioned as a source of information; libraries also, obviously, have a role to play here, either in providing the information themselves or advising where it might be found. Central libraries generally have a set of the standard bibliographies which can be consulted. Bibliographies are expensive to buy new since the print run is usually quite small and publishers have to charge a large amount to make the venture pay; they can also be expensive secondhand, since there is a steady demand for them. Size as well as price can be prohibitive - the British Library catalogue runs to some eight feet of large 4to volumes. Against this, some of the larger bibliographies are now being made available on CD-Rom.

VALUES

'I've got this old book I want to sell.'

'Let's have a look ...I'm afraid I don't think its worth very much.'

'Why not? Its old, isn't it?'

'Well, 1892 isn't that old, you know.'

'Over a hundred years? I call that old!'

'And you know, age alone doesn't make a book valuable.'

'What does then?'

'Oh, all sorts of factors ... But this sort of thing ... It just isn't saleable.'

'Why isn't it?'

'Because nobody wants it. There's no demand.'

'Well, what is saleable then?'

'...'

At some point, with luck, the phone will ring or a fire break out and the bookseller can break off the conversation. The customer will leave the shop in a state of high dudgeon, convinced the bookseller doesn't know his business. After a fruitless morning traipsing round half a dozen shops, he will be persuaded that the whole bookselling fraternity is in league to do him down.

The question of values of old books has been deliberately left towards the end. Anyone who has read this far will have some idea already of the factors affecting the value of particular copies; what remains to be faced is the question of what categories of books are valuable and which are not. This is a very large subject indeed. At the same time, perhaps paradoxically, it is not, in my opinion, a subject about which a great deal can be said, at least *usefully* said. What follows is a personal reflection upon the subject, with what I hope will be useful pointers to the uninitiated.

A distinction can be drawn between, on the one hand, an individual copy and a particular price, and on the other, books in general and their value. To talk about values is to generalise; the particular on which the generalisation is based is price. But how does one generalise about values over a field which ranges from paperbacks to uncunables? How does one generalise about values of what are, in many cases, unique items (two copies of a book are seldom identical in all respects, especially with regard to condition)? How does one cope with what may be termed the heirarchy of the trade? (Given that most booksellers spend most of their time buying and selling amongst themselves, the value of a given book will necessarily vary from one bookseller to another.)

It is much easier to talk about price: a particular copy of a book sold for, or was offered for sale, for a given amount in given circumstances at a given time. A large number of variables affect the price at which a given copy may sell, many of which have already been discussed; they include the condition of the book, the binding, the provenance, the presence of annotations. Fashion is another consideration; book collecting is as subject to the influence of fashion as any other field. A subject may be in fashion for some years and then go out of fashion, with an inevitable effect upon prices. Factors pertaining to the circumstances of the sale are also important, principally, how the book was sold. Was it in auction? If so, what type and who was present at the sale? Was it sold through a specialist catalogue? Or in a small out-of-the-way general shop? It is the existence of these and other variables which makes the transition from price to value so difficult.

The most that can usefully be done, and this only with books of some significance, is to establish a range of values, much as an auctioneer will give a lower and an upper estimate of what a book might fetch. But this is only an estimate, and liable to prove seriously inaccurate if the books appears on the market.

The simplest principle governing the values of secondhand books is the law of the market, of supply and demand. If there is a demand for the book, copies will have some value. The greater the imbalance between supply and demand, the greater the value. This fact, though easy to state, is not one readily grasped by many who approach their local bookseller full of hope with a box of miscellaneous books cleared from the attic or from a jumble sale. The book has to be wanted before the bookseller will consider making an offer at all. And with all his failings, the bookseller is almost certainly better qualified than the vendor to determine what is in demand and what is not, or, more specifically, what he can sell and what he cannot.

The would-be vendor should also be chary of taking the bookseller's price as a guide to what he is prepared to pay for a book or for a category of book, and this not only because the bookseller works on a margin significantly higher than is usual in the retail trade. Pricing a book and putting it on the shelf is not the same as selling the book. There is a sense in which every purchase the bookseller makes is speculative, a gamble; he doesn't *know* that the book he has just bought will sell, in the sense that the grocer knows he will sell so many pounds of butter over a given period (not least because people need butter but they don't need books). The nature of the business is such that the bookseller might have to wait a long time indeed - a matter of months or years - for the book to be sold. He might *never* sell the book! The slower the book is to sell (or the longer the bookseller has had a copy on his shelves) the more reluctant he will be to buy a second copy, even at a heavy discount to his asking price for his own copy. Conversely, if in the past the book has proved a ready seller, then the bookseller may be willing to pay well for a further copy.

It might be argued, from the point of view of conventional economics, that the reason the book does not sell is that it is priced too highly. Depite the fact that in a few cases this is undoubtedly true - there are a handful of booksellers who reverse the retailer's usual sales pitch: 'Never knowingly oversold' - in most cases it is not true. The bookseller makes a decision based on experience as to what price he can reasonably sell a book for. The problem of selling it then revolves around finding the customer who wants the book. A large reduction *may* attract an impulse buyer, or someone with only a slight interest in the subject matter of the book, but there is no guarantee. As like as not the book will remain unsold until the serious buyer makes an appearance, who is glad to buy the book at a price significantly less than he would have been prepared to pay!

I shall make what may appear to be bold statement, that the majority of secondhand books have little or no commercial value. While they may still be read, and even enjoyed, while they may still have *use value*, they do not have any exchange value. Put another way, for the majority of books there is little or no demand in the second-hand market. This is the single most important fact to grasp when considering disposing of a collection or accumulation of general books, important if only because many people believe that *all* books, regardless of age, subject matter and condition, have some commercial value. It is this belief which is exemplified in the dialogue with which the chapter opened.

Categories of 'unsaleable' books would include books that have outlived their function - old text books on astronomy, engineering, accountancy and medicine (but not, obviously, *antiquarian* books on the same subjects); novels of the 1920's, 30's and 40's by authors whom nobody is interested in today; religious tracts and texts with nothing to distinguish them from countless others; biographies of people who have long since passed from public notice. This is not say that occasionally, very occasionally, the bookseller might not be asked for a book which falls into one of the above categories. And if by some remote chance he is able to supply it he might expect to receive a pound or two.

Book club editions of almost any type and period are shunned, simply because they were published in such numbers. Books of verse likewise, firstly because the demand for poetry is slight and selective, secondly, because the supply, in terms of old editions is enormous. Wordsworth will sell in almost any edition, whereas John Greenleaf Whittier is unsaleable. Yet late nineteenth-century editons of the latter's works abound. Unfortunately, there are far more Whittiers than Wordsworths about.

Remainders are new books sold off by the publisher at a discount price. There are new bookshops in many high streets specialising in their sale. While a few secondhand bookshops do deal in remainders, the majority are very reluctant to handle them. There are far too many copies in circulation and the subject matter of the books is often too 'popular' for the secondhand trade. The market in secondhand books is very different from that in new books.

Then there are many eighteenth-century books, and earlier - pocket editions of standard authors, especially, usually in broken calf. To the untutored eye these may look interesting and potentially valuable, but again demand is neglible. The fact that they are 'old' is neither here nor there as far as value is concerned. They have nothing to recommend them as texts. They are not first editions, often not even early editions, but cheap reprints for the popular market, often on poor quality paper and in very small type.

These are just a few examples of the kind of book that I describe as of little or no commercial value; there are many, many more. But I am generalising, and all generalisations are hostages to fortune; there will always be an exception that tests the rule, the odd book that proves to be worth a significant sum. All I am trying to do is give a rough picture of the kind of book in which booksellers are least interested. The fact that in some bookshops you will see rows and rows of these and similar 'unsaleable' books does not make them saleable. The bookseller might have nothing better to fill part of the shop; he might not be able to bear throwing books away; he might hope for an occasional purchase by a browser for a modest sum. However, in most cases the books will have been acquired against the bookseller's will, in the sense that they came his way as a result of the purchase of a large collection, of which a proportion only had real interest and value. If a would-be vendor appears in the shop with a box of books of the type just described, the bookseller will almost certainly decline to buy them.

According to an old saw popular among booksellers there is a customer for every book, or to use the jargon already employed, there is a demand for every book. This may be true in theory but theory isn't much use when it comes to practical bookselling. There may be a potential customer out there somewhere, but the task of locating that customer and persuading him or her to buy the book at anything more than a nominal sum - nominal since, by hypothesis, demand for the book is almost non-existant - is just not an economic one.

Experience is the key to a knowledge of values. For the person new to secondhand bookshops much may appear interesting when seen for the first time. The first-time visitor may spend time browsing but is unlikely to spend money. The experienced collector, on the other hand, can very quickly appraise a bookshop's possibilities.

Above the mass of 'unsaleable' books circulating, or stagnating, on the secondhand market, there is another, thick layer of books which have a real if modest value, a matter of a few pounds or more. Books of this sort of value are generally bought by the box-full and not individually. Few booksellers will be prepared to spend any time haggling over the purchase of a single book which they might expect to sell for seven or eight pounds.

If a collection of such books is devoted to one subject - cricket, philosophy, theatre - there might be a market for them with a specialist dealer operating, as like as not, from home and by catalogue. If the collection is miscellaneous it is often described in the trade as 'shop stock'. Whether a particular bookseller is interested in buying a collection of shop stock depends on a number of factors - the quality of the books relative to their subject (eg., is the book the definitive scholarly work on its subject or a mere populariser; the quantity involved and their condition; the quantity of books he already has on the shelves; cash flow). If the books are not of a particularly high quality in the sense just referred to, or not in a field which is in demand and readily saleable, the bookseller may make a very low offer or none at all. With a continuing decline in the number of general secondhand bookshops the market for miscellaneous undistinguished shop stock is becoming ever more restricted - a buyer's rather than a seller's market.

The rather negative tone evident so far in this chapter is not designed to put the reader off buying, selling and collecting books, rather to adjust expectations to a level corresponding more or less to reality. Having, I hope, achieved this aim we can now consider that small proportion of old books which have some real and significant value.

What distinguishes such a book from the ruck? In very general terms the book will carry some weight, intellectual, artistic, scholarly or artistic. It will have made its mark, at the time of publication, in the field with which it deals, whether it be science, literature, philosophy, medicine, art, or any other area of human endeavour. (Alternatively, it may have been recognised as an important work only years after its publication.) The book will be the first edition or a very early edition. So we have the idea of the first or early appearance of an important book: Bronte's *Jane Eyre*, Wordsworth's *Lyrical Ballads*, Darwin's *Origin of Species*, Newton's work on gravity. So much may appear too obvious to be worth stating. But the same principle applies at a more humdrum level. Early books in almost any field will have some value: the first books treating of television or of computing; the first book detailing some advance in medical science; even, from a bibliographical point of view, the first books utilising a new design of type. As a general principle, the earlier the book relative to its subject matter the more likely it is to have some value (age alone generally doesn't bestow value).

The principle that the more important the book is in its field the more likely it is to have value applies not only to the obviously important works of the sort just cited but to the more obscure, the more specialist book, particularly within quasi-technical fields. A related rule of thumb which may be applied throughout many areas of book collecting concerns the size of the book relative to the subject matter: a quarto volume of 250 pages taking as its subject the country houses of England is, on balance, likely to be much less sought after than a book of the same format and page-length dealing with a single country house. The former is considerably less likely to contain information which can't be obtained elsewhere, while the latter may well be the definitive work on its subect.

Then there are categories within which almost any book will have at least a modest value: anything published in the fifteenth century; colour plate books of the eighteenth and nineteenth centuries; eighteenth-century travel in the Antipodes; nineteenth-century travel in the Caucasus; seventeenth-century cookery.

A discussion of what books are valuable merges into a discussion of what books are collectable, and since a later chapter is devoted to the latter topic I shall say no more about collecting categories now. In the end, no matter how many guide lines are devised and tips given, knowledge of values, as with knowledge of everything else, is only acquired through experience, through visiting shops and book fairs, through perusing catalogues and attending auctions, even through talking to professionals.

Once a book has been identified as being potentially of value, the particular copy to hand must then be examined to discover how valuable it may be in relation to its condition and state. Much has already been said on this subject in previous chapters. To recap: condition is of the first importance; a book in fine condition will usually be worth much more than a copy in poor condition. In betwen 'fine' and 'poor' there are many gradations of condition, and hence of value. 'Originality' has also been discussed at some length, meaning a book which is in a state as close as possible to that in which it was originally issued to the public by the publisher. Everything that the publisher and printer included in the book should be present if the copy is to command the highest price. Missing advertisments are an irritant; a missing blank leaf or half-title a further irritant. Anything else that might be lacking is often terminal as far as value is concerned. The book should preferably bear the original binding put on by the publisher, or in the case of leather-bound books, a contemporary binding.

Books that have been rebound at some point in their lives will generally command less money than one in an original or contemporary binding. Where a book was issued with a dust-jacket a copy without the jacket will almost certainly be worth less than a copy which retains it, even though the difference in many cases might be modest. With modern first editions the difference is often crucial. Many specialist booksellers won't even bother to handle a copy which lacks the jacket.

Provenance can be important - who has owned the book before and what marks of ownership they made. The simple signature of someone famous can add to the value of a book, if not create value where none would have existed otherwise. Annotations by a previous owner may add to the value, or they may detract considerably if by someone unknown and of an assinine nature. Provenance includes the idea of the association copy, a copy desirable because of an association with someone other than the author. A copy from a famous library or private collection will often command a higher price than a copy without that association.

Price Guides

There are three different types of reference work generally available which give information about prices and values (not the same thing) and which can be used as a guide by the interested collector. The first type purports to say what a particular book is worth - X pounds. An occasional difficulty with this type of information is that it sometimes isn't put into context, in the sense that it isn't obvious whether the figure given is what a dealer would pay and whether that dealer is a specialist or not, or whether it is the figure the private collector would expect to have to pay. Sometimes the guide makes it explicit that the figure represents a notional 'trade price' but the idea of a trade price itself needs to be treated with some caution. What one dealer will pay for a book is not necessarily what another will pay.

Sometimes this notional trade price is arrived at by a study of auction prices, in the form of an annual compilation called Book Auction Records, already mentioned in the chapter on Bibliographies. The advantage of this type of guide is that it at least indicates what was actually paid for a given copy of the book - the price is real rather than hypothetical. Book Auction Records summarise details of all individual books offered for sale in the preceeding auction season, roughly from September to July, at all the main auction houses in the U.K. and the U.S.A. as well as selected houses on the Continent and elsewhere. The records need to be treated carefully and some interpretation is generally necessary. Several entries for the same book (not the same copy) over a short period of time will give a better indication of value than a single, isolated entry. An apparently higher than average price for a book may be accounted for by the fact that the particular copy was an association copy or was in some other way distinguished; a lower than average price, by the fact that the copy was in poor condition. These distinguishing features are not always evident from the description in the records. Fashion is another factor to be taken into account. High prices for an author or for a type of book fashionable ten or more years ago may not be realisable today. Book Auction Records are quite expensive to buy new, though older volumes can often be picked up quite cheaply secondhand. Central Reference Libraries usually have a set on their shelves, not least because librarians themselves consult them.

The third type of guide consists of booksellers' own catalogues. This gives the price at which the bookseller thought he or she could sell a particular book, though it is only a price - there is no way of knowing whether the book was actually sold or not. Nevertheless, catalogues, particularly specialist catalogues, can provide an interesting and useful guide to the market. Collating the information can be somewhat tedious; the more specialist one's interests, the easier the information is to collate. It is merely a question of getting on the mailing list of the relevant specialist dealers. For someone with broad interests a large accumulation of catalogues will have to be scanned. Several publishers now produce annual compilations of such information, condensing the catalogue details of a number of more or less specialist dealers into an easily accesible form, so that a hunt through numerous separate catalogues to trace a particular item is replaced by a single check.

Auctions

There is a certain mystique attaching to auctions, engendered no doubt in part by the occasional snippet of television news recording the high drama of a lot sold for millions. For the working bookseller auctions are by and large a pretty humdrum affair, though the occasional sale of some especially notable library or collection is one of the pleasures of the business. Even during a run-of-the-mill country sale, where the lots are knocked down at an average of twenty or thirty pounds, with an occasional hundred or two, there is sometimes an unpredictable item, or one of unrecognised worth - unrecognised by the auctioneer, that is. As the bidding mounts through the hundreds the usual hum of conversation is stilled; an isolated cough disturbs the silence as it would in a theatre; heads turn to see who is bidding. As the first thousand is reached, dealers glance at each other with raised eyebrows; or with a knowing look, as much as to say, *they* knew all along what the lot was worth but didn't fancy going for it themselves. When the hammer finally falls there is - not applause; the professionals are too sophisticated for that - but an audible expulsion of air, a collective sigh, followed by a buzz of talk. And the room is rapidly brought down to earth when the following lot fails to sell for £15.

Auctions can be fun, even exciting. And for the tyro they offer one of the few opportunities to see booksellers actually buying books. The private customer has equal access to the auction, can buy the catalogue, can view the lots on offer, can form his or her own opinion as to likely selling price, and then watch the action, even participate.

The principle on which the auction *room* operates may as well be stated though it is doubtless familiar to most. A vendor *consigns* a book or a collection of books for sale. The auctioneer *lots* the books and catalogues them, generally providing a description of some sort. The auctioneer will probably suggest an *estimate* of what the books will fetch, that is a lower and an upper figure. Usually the estimate is printed in the catalogue against the entry, though some of the humbler auction rooms omit this. The auctioneer may suggest a *reserve*, that is, a minimum figure below which the item is not to be sold. This reserve, which is confidential, is usually just below the lower of the two estimates, though practice varies. When the lot comes up for sale the auctioneer accepts *bids* from the *floor*. If the lot is particularly important there may be a telephone bidder. One of the assistants relays the bidding over the phone to the person at the other end of the line. The auctioneer may have a number of *commission bids* to execute, that is, bids left with him by those unable or unwilling to attend the sale in person. Any reserve would in effect be a bid as well. With commission bids the auctioneer is under an obligation to secure the lot for the lowest amount possible compatible with other bids. A commission bidder may have left instructions for the auctioneer to go up to £300 on his behalf. If the last bid from the floor is £100, and there are no competing commission bids, the commission bidder should secure the lot at the next bid, £110 or £120. The *hammer price* is the price for which the lot is *knocked down* at the fall of the hammer. But the hammer price is not the price the buyer pays since there is added to it a *buyer's premium*. The average premium is currently ten percent. At the end of the sale the auctioneer will remit to the vendor the proceeds after deducting his commission.

The lot may, of course, fail to sell, either through not reaching its reserve or through not attracting a bid at all. In this case the lot will be *bought in*. It is often not obvious that a lot has been bought in. It is common practice for the auctioneer to call out the name of the purchaser after the fall of the hammer; the auctioneer may decide to use a fictitious name as a buying-in name. Many auctioneers print a list of prices realised at a given sale in the catalogue for their following sale; any lot numbers not listed represent lots that failed to sell or that were withdrawn from the sale.

The iron rule of auctions is *caveat emptor*. It is the buyer's responsibility to check for him or herself that the book in question is complete, whole and clean. The auctioneer accepts no responsibility in the matter, as the conditions of sale printed in the catalogue make clear. Notwithstanding this, many auction houses do agree to take back books which can be proved to be either seriously defective or not as described, but only if they form part of a 'named lot' as opposed to an anonymous item forming part of a collection of books, a shelf-full or box-load. If a lot is sold 'as seen' or 'with all faults' then it cannot be returned.

There exists, as already implied, a certain psychology of the auction room, of which the bidder should be aware. The general air of excitement may lead an inexperienced bidder to go higher than he or she intended. The phenomenon is not unlike gambling - 'just one more bid!' Then there is the openly competitive nature of the auction. A dealer may be reluctant to be seen to be publicly defeated by a rival and therefore bids more than is wise. The only safe procedure is to decide carefully beforehand just how much you are prepared to pay, always including the buyer's premium, and resolutely stop when the bidding reaches that point. It is a good idea to turn away from the auctioneer, to make it plain to yourself as much as to him that you are out of the bidding.

For a novice a dry run would be a good idea before attempting to buy at auction. Visit a few, on viewing days and sale days, to get the feel of the place before putting a toe in the water. The telephone directory will give details of local auctioneers and a call will tell if they handle any books. It would be advisable to gain a little experience with a small, local auction before moving onto the specialist auctions, not least because any mistakes made are likely to be relatively cheap ones.

A common misconception is that the auction price of a book represents its 'trade price'. There is some basis for this belief in as much as the majority of bidders tend to be in the trade. However, there are too many other possible scenarios for this to be taken as axiomatic. A dealer might be acting on behalf of a private client, in which case he is likely to bid much higher than he would if he were buying the book for stock. And private collectors do buy at auction, and if two are in competition then the price is likely to be driven far beyond any notional 'trade price'.

Book Fairs

The growth of the book fair has had a profound effect on the development of the secondhand book trade since the phenomenon really began to gather strength in the 1970's. The effects have not always been to the good of the trade or the buying public. (And there are many who assert that nowadays there are simply too many bookfairs being organised.) However, any deletorious effects are probably outweighed in most people's minds by the benefits which the development of the bookfair has brought in its wake.

Bookfairs range from a handful of stall holders gathered in a remote and draughty village hall offering cheap stock to a local public, to expensive West End venues attracting exhibitors and buyers from all over the country as well as from overseas. The typical fair is held at a weekend, in a central location in a provincial town or city, with anything between twenty and fifty exhibitors offering a wide range of stock from general secondhand to antiquarian.

Whatever the type of fair, the principle is the same: an individual, a company or organisation rents a hall, a room or exhibition space, invites booksellers to take a stall for a fee and publicises the event. Many bookfair organisers make a small charge for entry. (In the case of commercial organisations this money helps toward their profit margin, with non-profit-making organisations the charge helps to keep costs down. There are those who object to paying an entry fee, arguing by false analogy that they don't pay to go in to a shop. In many cases the costs of running a fair, principally the hire of the hall and advertising, are so great that if the full amount were charged to the exhibitors many would find the cost prohibitive and would not exhibit. The entry fee charged to the public therefore amounts to a small subsidy, helping to make the fair viable.)

Information about bookfairs can be obtained from the several trade organisations which promote them, from trade magazines and journals and from the local press. Many fairs have a table just inside the entrance carrying leaflets advertising similar events around the country.

The great advantage of the bookfair from the bookseller's point of view is that it allows him or her to show a selection of their stock to a potentially large number of people for a very modest outlay. It is undoubtedly the low overheads associated with the bookfair that have attracted many part-time booksellers into the field. Apart from the stand rent, the only initial expenditure is the purchase of a set of folding bookshelves. With a set of shelves, and stock to fill them, the tyro bookseller can contact the organiser of a fair, book a space at the next fair, arrive early on the day and set up for business. Many bookfairs, though, have their regular exhibitors who take priority when it comes to booking and newcomers may have to go on a waiting list. Fairs organised by trade associations are only open, naturally enough, to members of that association.

The very idea of the bookfair often generates controversy among collectors and, to a lesser extent, dealers. It is asserted that all the 'bargains' are snapped up by the exhibitors before the fair opens, leaving nothing for the general public. This assertion begs a number of questions. Firstly, what is a 'bargain'? Secondly, is the book-buying public only interested in bargains? One might also, if bargains are one's main interest, query the ability of the exhibitors to discover every one. I well remember a fair at which I exhibited. A few days afterwards I learnt of a book which had been bought for £5 several hours after the fair had opened and whose true value was nearer £500. Virtually every bookfair exhibitor could tell a similar tale.

It would be against human nature to expect exhibiting booksellers not to examine each other's stock as soon as possible - as the bookseller is putting the stock onto his or her shelves, or even before the books are out of their boxes. In fact, at a number of fairs there are booksellers who exhibit primarily with a view to what they can buy before the fair opens.

But this aspect of the fair should not put off the general public, nor even the 'visiting trade'. And in most cases it is obvious that it doesn't put them off. With the majority of fairs, trading between the exhibitors represents only a small proportion of the total amount of business transacted during the day.

For the novice collector, or for the person who hasn't even begun to think about collecting books, the great advantage of the bookfair is that it allows him or her easy access to a wide range of books which would otherwise be difficult to view. A majority of booksellers now operate from their home, and 'home' may be anywhere in the country. Viewing their stock could involve long journeys and entail a slight measure of embarrassment should the books prove too expensive or not what is wanted. With many shops the situation is not much better. The more valuable books are kept in locked cabinets, or are sometimes not on show at all but held in a special store room open only to the trade and known customers. At the bookfair, by contrast, all the books on offer are open to inspection without question by any visitor. Not only are the books open to inspection but the bookseller is often available to talk about the books, particularly in the afternoon, after the first rush has died down and time begins to hang a little heavy. Many exhibitors also see the fair as an opportunity to meet potential new customers for their catalogue trade, collectors who will become customers in the future.

The main beneficial effect of the bookfair phenomenon is that it has opened up the trade to a far greater number of people, both exhibitors, many of whom are part-timers, and visitors, many of whom would not normally enter a secondhand bookshop, supposing such a thing still exists in their vicinity. The most pernicious effect of the growth of the bookfair is, in my opinion, the encouragement it has given to haggling.

The promiscuity of the bookfair, with booksellers and private buyers congregating round the stall, overhearing each other's business, has inevitably led to an increase in bargaining, negotiating or haggling. It is assumed by many, usually wrongly, that the price marked in the book represents not what the bookseller expects for the book but the figure at which he or she is prepared to start haggling. Partly to blame is the practice of booksellers of offering an automatic discount of ten percent to fellow members of the trade, nowadays more as a courtesy than anything else. This practice has been standard in the trade for decades. What has changed of late, especially within the context of the bookfair, is that many booksellers themselves now expect more than ten percent, or at least hold out for more than that amount; the general public, becoming aware of this discounting, not unnaturally feels that they too should have the benfit of it. The result is what might be termed a general price instability, an assumption that every price in every book is negotiable. The first-time visitor to a fair should be aware that this is not so.

Given that the bookseller would offer a ten percent discount to fellow booksellers it isn't unusual for them to offer the same reduction to private buyers, but with many dealers this as far as the discounting goes. Attempts to negotiate a greater discount often result in a polite brush off. That is not say that a greater discount may not be available but that it would be entirely dependent on circumstances - the particular bookseller involved, how long he or she has had the book in question in stock, how much they paid for it, how well they know the would-be purchaser (if there is a well-established relationship the bookseller might offer a greater reduction as a gesture of goodwill). The marked price of the book is also important. The more significant the sum involved, the greater the degree of leeway the bookseller is likely to have.

The very worst approach, and one guaranteed to irritate any bookseller, is to 'make an offer' on a book priced at a pound or two, for the mere sake of haggling. I once had a customer who always argued for a reduction, whatever the marked price. On one occasion I sold him a book for £15 which I had marked at £20. A few months later I acquired a similar book which I knew would interest him and which I priced at £50. After some strenuous bargaining he eventually paid me £40 for it. The point of the anecdote is not whether the books were 'really' worth £20, £40 or £50 but that the customer didn't know or didn't care what was their real worth. He haggled as a matter of principle, a practice which I, in common with most booksellers, find extremely annoying. If he had been straightforward in his approach I would have priced, and sold, both books at £20.

In so far as one can give any advice on the subject of haggling I would suggest a cautious and tentative approach rather than an aggressive and patronising one. (I have in mind the kind of person who casually proffers the book to the bookseller and offers half the marked price while still perusing the shelves, not even bothering with the elementary courtesies.) Don't assume, on the basis of appearances, that the bookseller actually *needs* to make a sale at any price. It would be more tactful to plead poverty (the book is more than you can afford) than to claim that the book is too expensive (implying that the bookseller doesn't know his business). Be aware of the difference between a modest reduction offered as a gesture of goodwill and a large one which cuts into the bookseller's profit margin.

Catalogues

Over fifty percent of secondhand and antiquarian booksellers in the U.K. today do not conduct their business through a shop. Some will work through bookfairs, many sell books by mail. Some booksellers who still run shops also issue catalogues from time to time. There are almost as many different types and styles of catalogue as there are booksellers to issue them, ranging from the barely legible mimeographed sheet offering miscellaneous books at a pound or two through to expensive glossy productions offering selected antiquarian stock of the highest quality at the highest prices. Many catalogues are more or less specialist, even if only on price. Most catalogues are 'free on request'.

For the collector catalogues can be an important source of information - about what subjects are in demand and what books in demand within that subject and at what price. Catalogues also offer the collector in a specialist area the opportunity to buy books easily, if not always very cheaply. Instead of scouring shops and fairs to find books within his field, the collector can turn to the specialist dealer who has done the work for him, albeit at a price.

Catalogue booksellers can be traced through directories of secondhand booksellers, through the membership directories of the various trade organisations and through advertisements in specialist magazines and journals. Visits to shops and fairs will also yield useful information. Most catalogue booksellers are pleased to expand their customer base; however, producing and posting catalogues can be a heavy expense and the bookseller is apt to become a little frustrated if nothing has been heard from the prospective customer after receipt of half a dozen catalogues. If you don't think you are likely to place an order but would still like to continue receiving catalogues it would be courteous to offer to pay a small amount as a subscription.

Catalogues from specialist booksellers can be useful not only as a guide to prices but also, perhaps more interestingly, as a bibliographical guide to books in a given field. It is not surprising if a bookseller develops over the years an expertise in his or her own subject which makes them more knowledgeable than most; this expertise is often reflected in the catalogues they produce, making of them valuable reference tools. It is not unusual, after a lapse of time, to see catalogues of this calibre listed for sale in other booksellers' catalogues! General bookshops often have somewhere on the premises a box or two of miscellaneous ephemera which might contain a number of old catalogues. It is always worth rummaging through these boxes to see if they contain any catalogues of note; even if you are not interested in the subject they cover they may still prove useful at some future date. This is a very cheap way of beginning to accumulate a reference library.

Collecting Books

This book is called *Book Collecting* but so far little has been said overtly about the collecting of books. However, every topic that has been discussed is of relevance to the collector - the physical make-up of the book, format, paper, edition, condition, completeness, illustrative material and so on. Without at least a basic knowledge of such matters it is doubtful if there can be any such thing as 'collecting'. Collecting implies deliberation, intention, above all, it implies choice. And for that choice to be meaningful, it must be informed choice.

But what exactly is collecting? What distinguishes collecting from, say, buying books to read? The answer is implicit in the preceding paragraph; what is distinctive about the *collecting* of books is that the book as physical object is as important as the book as text, as means of conveying information. The collector is as interested, if not more interested, in the printing of the book, its typography, its binding, its illustrations, the particular edition, the provenance of a particular copy and, quite possibly, a host of other aspects. Almost any physical aspect of the book can be the subject of a collecting interest. Even the collector of modern first editions is primarily interested in the book as object. A 'second impression' may be identical to the first edition in all respects apart from the addition of those two words, but their addition makes the book a different object from the first edition.

I do not wish to assert that collectors do not read the books they buy - some of them certainly do. And for some collectors, the reading is still the primary satisfaction. Their intellectual interest may lie in ephemeral eighteenth-century pamphlets or obscure seventeenth-century poets; the fact that they collect them in original edition may simply be because there was never any other edition. But for some, the pleasures of reading are enhanced by the knowledge that they are reading a first, or otherwise important edition, rather than a mere reprint. There is a feeling of being closer to the author and his time. Whereas the 'mere' reader - and I do not mean to disparage reading - is interested primarily in the text for his or her own purposes, the collector will always give at least equal importance to considerations of originality and contemporaneity. (Some collectors do, of course, face an acute dilemma in this regard: can they afford to read their first editions, given the possibility of wear and tear, and consequent diminution of value?)

The book as object is one defining characteristic of book collecting; the second, as important, is the idea of theme. If the collection is to *be* a collection rather than a simple accumulation, there must be some unifying theme or idea behind the collection.

In 1965 the National Book League put on an exhibition called *Treasures fom Private Libraries in England.* Various distinguished collectors were asked to offer for exhibition a few books from their collections, and to provide a brief introduction for the catalogue. Cyril Connolly offered a very personal but at the same time illuminating view of book collecting in his contribution which he called 'Hommage to the Twenties, 1919-29':

'Collecting is a means of extracting order from chaos, of providing sanctuary for genius or survival for the unfittest, depending on the collector. *Sapientum templa serena!* Let us confine ourselves to those who erect shrines to human wisdom rather than saints' reliquaries. The principle is the same.

'At first I liked old books: only gradually did the design form to acquire in their original form all the works which constitute the modern movement in literature: French, English, American - over the last hundred years. A hopeless task and one which precludes specialization, as there is neither time nor room nor money to include all the variant issues and ten years' editing has given me a distaste for manuscripts of which I possess hardly any. My collection makes up in variety what it lacks in beauty in itself, a labour of admiration, it is constantly in use as a means of evaluation. No poet can be appreciated, for example, except through the original volumes, the slimmer the better, which record his progress ...'

In a completely different vein, we learn from the same catalogue of the beginnings of the Duke of Wellington's collection:

'... the chief treasures [of the library] came to him during the Spanish campaign - particularly at the battle of Vitoria. On that day, when the French left the field, the coach of Joseph Bonaparte was intercepted by British cavalry and the King barely escaped by mounting a horse. The captured coach was found to contain ... a number of very fine manuscripts. These were placed in the hands of the Duke who wrote to the legitimate King of Spain offering to return them. Ferdinand VII, however, asked the liberator of his country to keep them and, after a further exchange of letters, the Duke saw no reason not accede to the King's wishes.'

One might wonder whether the present upheavals in Eastern Europe will not provide the foundation for a private collection of material similarly 'exported' from its native home.

A hundred years ago serious book collecting was generally confined to books printed before the seventeenth century; fifty years ago the field had broadened to include much of the eighteenth and nineteenth centuries. Today the collecting field is extensive in the extreme. A hundred years ago the serious collector might concentrate on incunables; today, though there are still collectors of incunables to be found, there are far more people collecting nineteenth-century novelists, early Penguins, twentieth-century childrens' books or early motoring titles. For most of us, the cost of acquiring a collection of incunables is just too great; for some of us, the expertise may be lacking (though it could be acquired); for yet others, the interest may simply not be there. We each of us collect according to our background, our interests and our means. Value judgements *within* a particular field are constantly being applied (one copy of a book is in better condition than another; one edition is superior to another); but value judgements between distinct collecting fields are fairly meaningless.

All is grist to the mill of the collector, perhaps more so with books than with many other items of our cultural history since there are so many books about. Most books can be collected for one reason or another. It is up to the would-be collector to find a theme. (I once knew an eccentric who collected all books with red covers.)

What has struck me repeatedly over the years is the number of people who began collecting books in a casual way, sometimes so casual that their activity could hardly be said to constitute collecting, but yet who were gradually drawn into serious collecting by the discovery of some hitherto neglected aspect of their chosen field. The mere fact of collecting books possessing the relevant point itself brings that point into prominence and general recognition. Before very long, the collector finds him or herself in competition with a range of others who have taken up their enthusiasm, and the price of the books begins to rise!

A bookseller I once worked for began building a collection of every Penguin paperback ever published, long before anyone else had considered Penguins worthy of such attention. Soon his activities came to the notice of some of his customers, who 'discovered' Penguins as a collecting field and themselves began collecting early imprints or some of the sub-series. Before long there was established locally a Penguin Collectors' Club, with membership subscription and newsletter. Penguins had 'arrived'.

While there is an answer to the question, what is collectable? there is no answer, at least in specific terms, to the question, what to collect? Everyone must decide for themselves. The first question can be answered by listing exhaustively all those categories of books which constitute an established collecting field: nineteenth-century writers, colour-plate books, modern first editions, early childrens' books, early scientific and medical books, herbals, topography and travel, and so on. The second question can only be answered by the individual concerned. The only guidance I can offer is that the collecting field should reflect some genuine interest or enthusiasm.

If you can't bear Trollope, as many people can't, where is the fun in collecting first-edition Trollope? Trollope may be fashionable as a collecting interest and there may even be money to be made by laying down a collection of his first editions. But for excitement you would probably be better off speculating on the stock market. (I should perhaps say at this point that I have no advice to offer those who wish to collect for investment purposes, beyond suggesting that they put themselves in touch with a reputable bookseller and discuss the matter with them.) There are fashions in book collecting as there are in any other area of life but in my opinion they are best avoided. Fashion is especially noticeable in the area of modern first editions. In the 1920's the works of Galsworthy, G.B. Shaw and J.M. Barrie were highly collected. A decade later prices for their first editions had collapsed. Twenty years ago, first editions of P.G. Wodehouse were given scant consideration; nowadays they can fetch astronomical prices. It would be a brave collector who predicted that they will be just as high, in real terms, twenty years from now.

The theme of the collection may be of any nature. It may be strictly bibliographical - all books from a certain printer, all books with a certain typeface. An interesting field exploited by some is the collection of all the different editions of a particular work - *Robinson Crusoe*, Aesop's *Fables*, Gilbert White's *Natural History of Selborne*. There are those who collect types of binding, and not necessarily fine bindings at great cost but, for example, Victorian decorated cloth bindings or nineteenth-century printed paper wrappers.

Those with an interest in printing may consider collecting books from **private presses**. These are books issued, usually in limited numbers, by a small privately-owned press whose interest is as much in fine printing as it is strictly commercial. Such books are generally hand-set and hand-printed on hand-made paper, with special attention paid to the binding as well. To some extent the rise of the private press towards the end of the nineteenth century may be seen as a reaction to the dominance of machinery in general printing and a perceived loss of quality in the end product.

William Morris's Kelmscott Press, established in Hammersmith in 1891, is one of the most famous private presses, with editions of Chaucer and Shakespeare, as well as of Morris's own works and of those writers and artists associated with the Pre-Raphaelite movement. The Kelmscott Press was succeeded by the Doves Press, established by T. Cobden-Sanderson in 1898. The Doves Press printed works by some of the most important writers of the nineteenth century - Goethe, Browning, Wordsworth, Keats and Ruskin - as well as editions of Shakespeare and, perhaps most famously, an English Bible. All of these editions were limited; the Doves Press was noted for printing within each edition a very small number of copies - perhaps ten or twelve - on vellum. The Golden Cockerell Press was founded in 1921, and during the following forty years printed some hundreds of editions of writers contemporay and classic - T.E. Lawrence, H.E. Bates and H.G. Wells as well as Ovid, Aesop and Gawain and the Green Knight - usually in two editions, one of up to 100 copies and a second in an edition of several hundred.

The private press still flourishes today, though in a much more diversified form. While prices for productions of the older presses can be very high, those for works published by modern presses are often still within the means of most.

For those whose interest is mainly literary, the collecting theme may be a single writer - from ancient to modern - or group of writers whose work has something in common, for example, writers of the 1890's, Wilde, Beardsley, Housman, Le Gallienne, Henry Newbolt. The theme may be women writers of the eighteenth or nineteenth centuries, or both; it may be minor poets of the eighteenth century (since all the major poets are already collected and expensive in first edition). This latter field, it has to be said, is already being worked, though there is still room for others to set their hands to the plough. What is particularly interesting about this and similar fields is the manner in which minor authors may be 'discovered' by the universities; what was once seen as a minor talent may come to be seen as something more than that.

An element of social history may be injected into the collecting. Early and important works in the history of political movements - socialism, Marxism, trade unionism, fascism. Perhaps more entertaining, certainly more lightweight, would be a collection of 'railway literature' of the nineteenth century, given that the development of the railway system stimulated significant changes in publishing practice and the retail distribution of books, particularly fiction.

The collecting may be of a series of publications issued in uniform format. I have already mentioned Batsford publications and Penguin paperbacks. There are many others, mainly but not exclusively confined to the twentieth century: guide books of various types published by Baedeker, Ward Lock and A. & C. Black; King Penguins, Collins' *New Naturalist* series, A. & C. Black's 'colour books', Wisden's cricket annuals.

Series collecting might be focused on a particular publisher, such as John Camden Hotten, active in the second half of the nineteenth century and publisher of a good number of books on curious, out-of-the-way subjects but also a man of discernment and some courage, being the first to persevere with the works of Swinburne. A publisher of a completely different colour was Bernard Tauchnitz, whose publishing firm in Leipzig issued English editions for Continental sale of almost all the important contemporary writers of the nineteenth and early twentieth centuries.

The theme may be very general, such as childrens' books with its many subdivisions, roughly coextensive with the centuries, eighteenth, nineteenth and twentieth. Sport is another large theme, one generally broken down into

W. H. Smith & Son's Subscription Library,

186, STRAND, LONDON.

Messrs. W. H. SMITH & SON beg to call the attention of the Nobility, Gentry, and Residents in the Country to their new Subscription Library, established in connection with their numerous Railway Bookstalls, thus affording to Subscribers all the advantages of the London Libraries—with the additional advantage of a continual exchange of books free of further charge.

This Library is intended to promote the reading of the higher class of Literature, as issued from the London Press, embracing all the most important works in Art, Biography, History, Travel, Fiction, Poetry, Science, Theology, &c.

The Terms of Subscription, commencing at any date, and paid in advance, either at the Railway Bookstall, or 186, Strand, London (without any additional charge for carriage), are—

	6 Months.		12 Months.
For *One* Volume at a time....	£0 12 6	—	£1 1 0
For *Two* Volumes „	1 0 0	—	1 11 6
For *Three* „ „	1 7 0	—	2 2 0
For *Six* „ „	2 2 0	—	3 3 0
For *Twelve* „ „	3 3 0	—	5 5 0

A small selection of Books will be kept at the Principal Bookstalls, where the Subscribers may exchange at pleasure, and the Clerk in charge will obtain from the London House, without delay, any that may not be in stock at the Station.

Subscribers, however, are requested to observe that they will be able to exchange Books *only* at the Station at which their Subscriptions are paid; but they may, by advising the London House, from time to time transfer the place of exchange to any other locality where a Bookstall is established.

Subscribers residing near a Railway Station where no Bookstall is established, will be required to pay the carriage to and from the nearest Depôt. In these cases two days must be allowed for exchange.

Terms for Literary Institutions, &c., can be had on application to 186, Strand, London.

An advertisement for W.H. Smith's Subscription Library, mid-nineteenth century.

The development of the railway system in the nineteenth century had a significant effect upon publishing practice and the nation's reading habits, especially with the expansion of the subscription library. Such libraries made a charge per volume and were responsible for maintaining the tradition of the three-decker novel instituted by the circulating libraries of the early nineteenth century. A three-decker is a novel issued in three separate volumes. This practice allowed the library to charge for three volumes instead of one.

single sports or a small group. A particular aspect of a given sport may be selected - fly-fishing as opposed to fishing in general, or fly-tying as opposed to fly-fishing in general!

More general still is the field of illustrated books, or books with pictures in them. Here the field ranges from early woodcut illustrations of the fifteenth century to twentieth-century wood-engravings. The field is so vast that the only advice I offer is to explore thoroughly before settling on an area, to spend time in shops and at fairs looking at different illustrators and types of illustration, deciding what you like and what you can afford.

A glance through a directory of booksellers reveals specialists in books on bees, on women aviators, on sheepdog trials, gypsies, Christmas, Arthuriana, the laws of chance and the history of computing. All these, and other esoteric specialisms, we may suppose correspond more or less to the interests of at least a handful of collectors. What is collected is a matter for the individual; the important point always to bear in mind is that the collecting should be fun, if not exciting. And for it to be exciting it needs to be fed by a genuine interest in the subject on the part of the collector. If your hobby is angling, collect books on angling. If you work as a computer programmer, collect books on computing (though you may decide you don't want to be reminded of work). The idea of a pre-existing personal interest is important; it can also be profitable. The collector with specialised knowledge is quite likely to know more about a subject than many booksellers and will therefore have a better idea of which books are important in the field and which are not. This would apply particularly in many scientific and technical fields.

Once a field has been chosen, the principles on which the collection is to be based need to be sketched out, if not on paper then at least in the mind, so the collector knows in general terms how he or she intends to proceed. The ground rules will vary according to the subject chosen. With an author- collection most collectors would lay down as a minimum a copy in first edition of every book the author published. With a scientific writer the collector might decide that it was necessary to possess a copy of later editions as well, if they contained significant additions or alterations to the first. For collectors of modern firsts, only the first edition will do, as a matter of definition. Collectors of the works of literary figures may then decide that they need to have copies of the books to which their chosen author contributed prefaces, forewords and the like, as well as any anthologies in which their work appears. If they are really ambitious, and rich, their enthusiasm might extend to the manuscripts.

For those collecting in a general field some selectivity may well be necessary. The broader the field, the greater the degree of selectivity. By contrast, with the example of fly-tying cited above, it may be assumed that the total number of books on the subject is small and the collector can set himself the goal of acquiring a copy of every one without the risk of crowding himself out of house and home.

Having considered what is involved in collecting and also what the subject of the collection might be, the third and final question is, how to set about it? Whatever the collecting interest, indeed, even without any specific interest in mind, the only way to begin is by familiarising oneself with books of all sorts and values, by getting immersed in the subject. There is no substitute for direct, personal experience - handling different types of book, in different shops, gauging condition and rarity, comparing prices. The acquisition of some expertise, a familiarity with old books, is a *sine qua non* of all collecting. Futhermore, whatever one's particular enthusiasm, there is nothing to be lost, and often much to be gained by extending the scope of one's investigations into books in a variety of fields.

By spending time in shops and fairs, probably also by by requesting catalogues from specialist dealers, the novice collector will discover where the books in his or her chosen field are to be found and most easily, who the specialist booksellers are in that field, the price range between different booksellers, the jargon and abbreviations commonly employed and the standards different booksellers apply in matters of condition. The more specialised the interest, the easier is this process of familiarisation. The specialist booksellers are quickly located through directories and by word of mouth, and the eager novice will soon find him or herself in receipt of catalogues and quotations. The bookseller does not exist who does not need new customers.

Further Reading

The literature on the subject of books and bibliography is vast. Most of it is more or less specialist. Bibliographies proper have already been discussed in the chapter on the subject. What follows here are details of a few works which will be of general interest to one who wants to pursue the subject further. Virtually every book on the subject of books itself contains an appendix on 'further reading'; so by starting with one book, and taking note of the books so listed, the interested reader will be led gradually - some might say insidiously! - deeper and deeper into the subject. Most of the books listed here are either still available new, or are quite common secondhand.

A LIST OF BOOKS ABOUT BOOKS:

1. *Books about Books: Catalogue of the Library of the National Book League*, 1955.

ON PRINTING AND THE MAKING OF BOOKS:

2. S.H. Steinberg, *Five Hundred Years of Printing*, 1955.
3 Douglas C. McMurtrie, *The Book. The Story of Printing and Bookmaking*, republished 1989.

ON THE HISTORY AND MANUFACTURE OF TYPES:

4. D.B. Updike, *Printing Types. Their History, Forms and Use*, 1922.
5. Talbot Baines Reed, *The Old English Letter Foundries*, 1887.

ON THE PRINCIPLES OF TYPOGRAPHY:

6) Oliver Simon, *Introduction to Typography*, 1945.
7) Stanley Morison, *The Typographic Arts*, 1949.
(Morison wrote extensively on many aspects of books and all his works are well worth reading.)

On modern book production in general:

8. Hugh Williamson, *Methods of Book Design. The Practice of an Industrial Craft*, 1956.

On technical bibliography:

9. R.B. McKerrow, *Introduction to Bibliography for Literary Students*, 1927.
10. Phillip Gaskell, *New Introduction to Bibliography*, 1972
(Somewhat supersedes McKerrow.)

A scholarly book on technical terms:

11. Fredson Bowers, *Principles of Bibliographical Description*, 1986.

A popular A to Z of terms and expressions:

12. John Carter, *ABC for Book Collectors*, 1952 and since revised.

On book bindings:

13. John Carter, *Publishers' Cloth, 1820-1900*, 1935.
14. Michael Sadlier, *The Evolution of Publishers' Binding Styles, 1770-1900*, 1930.
(And other works by both Sadlier and Carter)

On book illustration:

15. David Bland, *The Illustration of Books*, 1951.
16. F.J.H. Darton, *Modern Book Illustration in Great Britain and America*, 1931.

On the Dust-Jacket:

17. Charles Rosner, *The Growth of the Dust-Jacket*, 1954.

On publishing history:

18. H.S. Bennett, *English Books and Readers, 1475-1557*, 1952.
19. F.A. Mumby, *Publishing and Bookselling: A History from the Earliest Times to the Present Day*, revised edition 1954.
20. James J. Barnes, *Free Trade in Books. A Study of the London Book Trade since 1800*, 1974.

Index

List of Advertisers